FIGHT YOUR
DARK SHADOW

Managing Depression with Cognitive Behaviour Therapy

by

Therrie Rosenvald

Tian P.S. Oei, Ph.D, FAPS

Illustrated by
Marco Schmidt

Cover Design by Marco Schmidt © 2007

Published by
depressionmanaged.com
24 Wallace Road
Beachmere, Queensland, 4510, Australia

Authors' Note

This book has been a joint effort of Therrie Rosenvald, Tian P.S. Oei and Marco Schmidt.

Tian P.S. Oei is a Professor of Clinical Psychology, School of Psychology at the University of Queensland, Brisbane, Australia. He is also the director of the CBT (Cognitive Behaviour Therapy) Unit at Toowong Private Hospital, Toowong, Brisbane, Australia. The CBT Unit runs Cognitive Behaviour Therapy workshops for people struggling with depression. CBT is one of Professor Oei's specialties and he has published more than 230 scientific papers and books on the subject.

I am a former journalist and this book started after I attended a CBT workshop at Toowong Private Hospital. I have been diagnosed with Major Depressive Disorder and have lived with depression for most of my life. We decided to write this book based on my experience as a sufferer of depression with scientific information provided by Professor Oei. In order to make the contents easier to understand, the messages are visualised in uplifting cartoons and illustrations. Marco Schmidt, graphic artist and cartoonist, produced all the illustrations, graphics and designed the layout and cover of the book.

We hope that you enjoy the book and that it gives you an insight into depression and how to overcome the problem.

Therrie Rosenvald
Tian P.S. Oei
Marco Schmidt

Brisbane, Australia, January 2007

Contents

Foreword

Disorders of mood are amongst the most distressing and debilitating conditions presenting to medical practitioners. They are also amongst the most common. As a psychiatrist, most of my working day is spent assisting those unfortunate enough to suffer a mood disorder. Many people think mood disorders are just disorders of emotion. However, I would encourage you to think beyond the emotional symptoms. Mood disorders primarily generate emotional suffering, but they also result in changes in thinking, judgement, behaviour, functioning and health. Often, the consequences of depression can be more debilitating than the symptoms themselves. There are numerous biological, psychological and social consequences, including: deteriorated physical and mental health and well-being; lost employment, finances or relationships; an altered self-concept; habitual helplessness; and suicide. Anything that can be done to alleviate the symptoms, the episodes, their functional impact and/or the longer term consequences must be done. Make no mistake; depressive disorders are lethal conditions for some, but chronic, burdensome, recurring, and disabling for the majority.

So what can be done? Frankly, quite a lot, which is, I hope, of some comfort to you. You may have cause to pick up this book because you or someone dear to you is suffering with a depressive condition of some type. It may be because you feel compelled or encouraged to seek out ways of assisting yourself. It may be because you know cognitive therapy is an effective intervention for all but the most severe depression, usually in combination with the necessary medication that your condition may indicate. This book represents an introduction to a therapeutic tool many have found useful. Whatever your reasons for reading on, I would encourage you to keep in mind why you want to get better: such motivations will always be of assistance, especially during the more difficult times.

Medical treatments will be discussed with you by your treating physician. These treatments will usually include, at least initially, medication. Antidepressant medication will usually be necessary for anything more than mild depression. Your physician will also explain about depression, its causes and treatments, and how you will be likely to progress over time. Psychological therapies provide additional benefit, and sometimes a person elects to pursue psychological treatment first, before any medication. Although the risks and benefits of this approach warrant discussion, it is ultimately your choice. I would always encourage you to consider the opinion of the appropriate medical experts when it comes to managing your mood. And I would encourage you to explore all reasonable avenues to assist your recovery.

In practise, I find that those that do best are those that are willing to do all that they can to assist recovery: those with motivation, enthusiasm for direct involvement in their management and a willingness to accept the problem and make the necessary changes to both their thinking and their environments. This is, not surprisingly, exactly what the scientific research in this area tells us.

Cognitive therapy is a type of psychological therapy that encourages awareness of how we may inadvertently contribute to our own depression. It provides a meaningful framework through which we can gain some understanding of ourselves and how we process our thoughts, feelings and surroundings. Cognitive therapy also then provides us with the necessary interventions, or "tools", to alter our perceptions and thoughts, which in turn reduces our distress and limits any impact on our underlying mood. I find that people then feel some sense of control over their mood, and therefore approach not only their depression, but also their lives, with a renewed sense of confidence, vigour and control.

Within these pages lies a simple and straight-forward introduction to the principles and processes of cognitive therapy. It is an introduction that I am sure you will find easy to understand, as it is written so that even someone with a significant depressive episode will be able to manage. The illustrations assist memory and understanding without detracting from the seriousness of the underlying condition. For you, it may be that this book sheds light onto the processes underlying mood and thereby allows you to adjust some of those processes to better assist your mood. Or, it may be a springboard for you to enter more formally into cognitive therapy. Either way, I hope for you that here begins a journey into recovery.

Dr Jon-Paul Khoo MBBS FRANZCP, Consultant Psychiatrist

This book is dedicated to all those who
are struggling with their moods
and those who care for loved ones
suffering from depression.

Introduction

Living with depression is at the best of times a struggle and at the worst of times it can be so debilitating that the pursuit of everyday activities are made nearly impossible. Depression causes us to fear life. It whips up an emotional dust storm and all we can see is a mass of grey matter surrounding us. There are no distinct features to focus on and nothing to give us some direction. Depression can become all consuming and there are times when it seems so much easier to just give in to the depression and let ourselves slide deeper into the emotional hole.

Even if our depression is mild it will have an adverse effect on our life and our environment. When suffering from depression we sometimes mistakenly believe that we are its only victim. Our depression has a negative influence, either directly or indirectly, on our partners, our children, our friends and even our work colleagues. Therefore learning to manage our depression is not only important for our own wellbeing but also for the wellbeing of those close to us.

Statistics show that most people will suffer some form of depression at some stage in their lives. It has been predicted that depression is fast becoming the number one mental health problem of the 21st century and countless working days are lost every year due to the effects of depression. Although depression is such a common problem it is still widely misunderstood by the general public. Despite the fact that government health departments and mental health organisations are trying to raise awareness and understanding of depression, there is still a stigma attached to it. Many people believe, especially sufferers, that depression occurs because of a personal failing or incompetence. Ignorance and misconceptions foster the 'blame-the-victim' attitude, which is unfortunately still widespread and pushes sufferers further into isolation.

The main aim of this book is to inform, in layman's terms, about depression. In the first part we point out what your role and responsibility is in the healing process of your depression. We go on to explain the different types of depression, the characteristics of the most common form of depression and the options you have in dealing with it. There is a section on medications, which have been highly successful in treating depression.

You may be familiar with the phrase "You are what you think". Cognitive Behaviour Therapy (CBT), which is one of the most successful therapy methods used today in the treatment of mental health problems, takes this statement one step further: "You **FEEL** what you think". In this book we describe where our negative thinking patterns originate from and how they influence our emotions. It shows how we can change them into positive patterns by applying the principles of CBT. This book helps you to recognise problems and work towards their solution, build up self-esteem, establish support systems and minimise the chances of relapsing into depression.

This book is aimed at people who may feel that they could be suffering from depression or have some problems with their moods. It can help you to decide whether or not you should seek medical advice. If you have been diagnosed with depression, this book will help you better understand your moods, why you feel this way and give a clearer picture of your treatment plan. This book is also a guide for people who are caring for depressed loved ones or have family or friends who suffer from depression. It will help them understand what the sufferer is going through and how they can be more supportive.

We must point out that this book is **NOT** meant as a means to self diagnose whether or not you are suffering from depression. Only a qualified physician or mental health professional can accurately make a diagnosis of depression. If you have the same or similar symptoms as described in this book we urge you to seek professional advice. Sometimes there are underlying medical reasons that have some of the same or similar symptoms as depression. This book does **NOT** replace therapy. It serves as an aid to your treatment plan.

However, you don't need to suffer from depression to benefit from this book because it can also simply help you to get to know your strengths, your weaknesses and limitations, as well as yourself, better. The methods of CBT are valuable lifestyle skills and it has been suggested that CBT should actually be taught in high schools as part of the curriculum. CBT is a tool that will assist you when dealing with the demands of everyday life. The strategies of CBT will help you stay healthy and focused when going through stressful times. The hectic lifestyle of today places many demands on our mental and physical stamina and you might agree that we can all do with a little extra help.

We have deliberately kept this book short and simple and each section is supported by illustrations that help you to understand the message better. There are some simple tasks you can do to identify your problem areas better. Even though this is a serious subject and dealing with depression is certainly no laughing matter, we have tried to bring some uplifting humour into our illustrations.

Depression can follow us around like a dark shadow, ever present and getting bigger all the time if we don't do anything about it. We hope this book can serve as a useful tool to fight the dark shadow of depression in your life.

* * *

The Right Toolkit

To deal with depression effectively we need the right tools. It's no use trying to hammer a nail into the wall with a saw. Even if we do manage to knock it into the wall a bit, it will never hold, nor be able to carry the weight of a picture. The same applies when dealing with depression. Telling yourself, or someone who has depression, to snap out of it or pull yourself together might work for three minutes, but in the long run it's not going to hold the negative feelings at bay. We need something that will last the distance and can be applied even when our emotional stamina is at its lowest.

This book aims to give us the right toolkit, so that **WE CAN** take charge and start to manage our depression and our problems more efficiently. In this book, we take an active approach and show how to use new skills in many different ways. You will develop knowledge on how to identify and cope with situations that exacerbate your depression. You will learn to implement strategies to help you deal with and overcome problems. These skills are not only for use in the short-term. They are long-term life skills that will help you in any situation you may face. It is likely that you will use these techniques for the rest of your life and that the more you use them, the better you will manage. These tools will help you to function at your full capacity and to enjoy a more fulfilling life.

With the right tools depression can be managed.

Taking the Mystery out of Mental Health Problems and Being in Control of our Treatment

To many of us the mere mention of the words psychiatry or mental health brings up images of being cookoo, brainwashed and subjected to some draconian mental health methods from the bad old days. Both Psychology and Psychiatry have come a very long way in the last 50 years and in today's psychiatric hospitals, the focus is on treating patients with respect and helping them regain their independence and emotional balance.

Treatment of mental disorders is not something that is **DONE TO US** and our doctor and health workers will not try to speak to us in complicated riddles, or try to keep us in the dark. On the contrary, openness in diagnosis and treatment is now considered vital for a successful outcome. **WE** are the only ones who have direct access to our mind and emotions, and **WE** have control over our treatment. In a sense **WE** become the physician and our doctor acts as our guidance counsellor. Therefore the better **WE** understand our mental health problems and treatment, the easier it will be to manage them and hopefully overcome them.

Under the guidance of your doctor you have to do the work to fight depression.

15

Making a Contract with Ourselves

Now that we know that we are in control of our own healing, we can look more closely at what is expected of us. When someone is depressed, they are often tempted to let someone else take charge, someone like a therapist, a doctor, or even a loved one. Confronting depression effectively means that **WE** have to roll up our sleeves and do the work ourselves. We are our own project and by working to help ourselves, we are making a commitment to ourselves; in effect we are entering into a contract with ourselves.

The key to managing our depression is within us, **NOT** in other people's behaviour, or even in our life circumstances. **WE ARE** the solution to our problems; no one else has the key to our inner workings. For our emotional and mental well being, it is vital that we start treating ourselves as the most important person in our life and be kinder and gentler towards ourselves. If we look after ourselves we can better look after those who depend on us. If we neglect ourselves we are not the only person who will suffer. Our family and our friends will feel the negative effect. Making a contract with ourselves will help us to focus on our wellbeing, instead of our shortcomings. Before long we will be sending out positive vibes, instead of negative ones.

Making a deal with yourself is taking responsibility for yourself.

We Have the Responsibility for Our Healing

If we look at our depression as a problem, rather than an illness, we can externalise it and thus it becomes something outside ourselves. This allows us to step back and examine it from different angles objectively. However, if we treat our depression as an illness, we internalise it and soon we will identify ourselves with it. It will become part of us and will be so much harder to dislodge. It also puts us in a passive role, and we will expect our doctor, (or other health professional) to take control. They are doing something **TO US** to treat the illness. This type of philosophy leads to the idea that we can get well, without having to actually do much work ourselves. It promotes the idea that it is someone else's responsibility, (usually our doctor's), to make us better. We hand over authority for our treatment in the hope that the illness will be cured. With depression this passive process can really limit the likelihood of a positive outcome.

On the other hand, if we consider our depression to be a problem (and not an illness), it will empower us to do something about it. This is different because it is an active, rather than a passive, concept. It is the attitude that **WE** have to do something about our depression and **WE** are the ones who can implement procedures and take steps to solve the problem. This requires us to **ACTIVELY** participate in the process of getting better. Managing depression is our responsibility and we have to take the authority to do something about it.

A)If you see depression as an illness it becomes part of you and it hinders you.
B) If you look at depression as a problem it is outside of yourself and
you can deal with it more effectively.

17

Controlling the Depression Beast

If we work at our depression what are the short-term and long-term outcomes we can expect? When treating depression, most mental health professionals prefer to concentrate on managing the problem, rather than finding a cure for the problem. This is because having an expectation that there is a complete and simple cure for depression can be unrealistic and therefore unhelpful. In reality, once depression gets a grip on us, it has a disruptive effect on every aspect our life. Therefore, we need to concentrate to slowly loosen the grip that depression has on us, by learning to "control the beast", not "cure the beast". The long-term outcome is: the better we learn to control our depression the more it will dwindle. Eventually, we will look at things that used to cause us depression as problems, which can be dealt with and that are a normal part of everyday living.

But treating depression is not as simple as just applying a band-aid onto a wound. It can sometimes be a long process. This process cannot be rushed and usually any attempts to take "shortcuts" just ends up backfiring. So it is best to take one step at a time, and to gradually understand and learn the methods of Cognitive Behaviour Therapy. In time this new way of thinking will become second nature. Although depression may want to raise its ugly head occasionally, after learning these new skills, we will soon be strong enough to curb the power it has had over us.

When we learn to control our depression beast it will start to disintegrate.

Different Types of Depression

Now that we know what our role is in the healing process and what we can expect to achieve we can look at this depression problem more closely. What is it? How does one feel and behave when having a problem with depression? Although most of us term anything from a minor emotional upset to a long drawn out feeling of sadness as depression, mental health professionals do differentiate between normal emotional distress and a pathologically altered mood. Also, to further assist in understanding depression, a distinction is made between different types of depression, sometimes referred to as "depressive disorders". The categorisation of each disorder is based on a manual which is called "The Diagnostic and Statistical Manual of Mental Disorders-Fourth Edition-Text Revision" also known as the DSM-IV-TR*.

Attaching diagnostic labels to people has been the subject of much debate among health professionals and the general public. On the negative side, it has been suggested that once labeled, some people may identify solely with the label and have difficulty overcoming it. For example, people labeled with "depression" may just come to accept it as a given fact and stop trying to work towards recovery. However, on the positive side, many people are relieved to find out that their symptoms actually have a name. They feel less isolated and feeling less isolated helps them to have hope. It is no longer just something they alone have experienced. They can learn more about their depression, its causes and how to overcome it. Knowing their depression empowers them and gives them a sense of personal control over it.

*The Diagnostic and Statistical Manual of Mental Disorders- Fourth Edition-Text Revision, DSM-IV-TR, is the current reference widely used in many countries by mental health professionals and physicians to diagnose mental disorders. The American Psychiatric Association publishes the Diagnostic and Statistical Manual of Mental Disorders. Since its first publication in 1952 it has gone through several revisions. The most recent version is the fourth edition. The current DSM-IV-TR lists over 200 mental health conditions and the criteria required for each one in order to make an appropriate diagnosis. The DSM-IV-TR is much more than just a diagnostic tool. Mental health professionals and physicians use it as a guide to communicate about mental health disorders. Furthermore the DSM-IV-TR is an educational tool and used as a reference for conducting all types of research such as clinical trials, prevalence studies and outcome research.

1) Major Depressive Disorder — Alternating Up and Downs

The most widely occurring form of depression is Major Depressive Disorder. According to the DSM-IV-TR, Major Depressive Disorder, also known as clinical depression, or unipolar depression, is described as feeling good for a period of time, then falling emotionally into a hole. Major Depressive Disorder affects different people in different ways. Some find it extremely hard, or even impossible, to function in their daily lives and workplaces. Others put on a 'brave face' and function reasonably well, and often on a very high level, in their careers and in front of other people, while deep down they feel depressed and disinterested in life. Most sufferers will have depressed moods and general loss of interest in activities they once enjoyed.

After being in a down-mode for maybe weeks, months or even years, sufferers can gradually start to feel good again, or at least much better. This pattern represents a depressive episode, with subsequent complete (or partial) recovery, which is often referred to as "remission". The DSM-IV-TR counts the first depressive episode, usually, as episode one and any following episodes are considered reoccurring if they happen within a two-year period of the first episode. The course of a recurrent Major Depressive Disorder differs from person to person. Some people have isolated depressive episodes interspersed with long periods without any symptoms. Others have a cluster of depressive episodes with short periods of remission in between. In the early stages of the disorder, the periods of recovery (i.e. remission) last longer. As the depression progresses, and when no treatment is sought, the good intervals will be shorter and the depressive episodes longer. The frequency of the episodes may increase with age.

Whether a person will suffer subsequent depressive episodes in the future depends on how many episodes have occurred in the past. The DSM-IV-TR rates that 50-60% of individuals who have suffered a single depressive episode can expect to have another one and the likelihood of a third episode increases up to 70% after the second episode and up to 90% after the third episode. Put simply, this means that as the number of depressive episodes experienced increases, so does the probability that the depression will only partially remit (i.e. it becomes less and less likely that full remission will occur, or last).

A depressive episode is considered to have ended if the symptoms have not occurred for at least two (2) consecutive months. The DSM-IV-TR states that in about 60% of cases, the depressive episode ends completely, meaning that none of the symptoms have occurred for at least two consecutive months (i.e. full remission). But, in one third of the cases, the depressive episode ends only partially (i.e. partial remission), or not at all. Because of this, it is sometimes difficult to distinguish between one episode and the beginning of the next episode.

Major Depressive Disorder can begin at any age; however, the average age it begins, is in the mid-twenties. According to the DSM-IV-TR, most sufferers are in the 25-44 year age group and the risk of developing Major Depressive Disorder is higher for women than for men. For preteen children, the risk of being affected by a Depressive Disorder is equal for boys and girls.

As Major Depressive Disorder is the most common type of depressive disorder, we have listed the symptoms associated with Major Depressive Disorder separately in our chapter "Symptoms of Depression".

NEED PROFESSIONAL HELP?
It is highly advisable that persons who suffer, or are suspected of suffering, from Major Depressive Disorder seek professional help. Under the guidance of a health professional, the chances of controlling the disorder are good. This disorder is associated with a high mortality rate. Up to 15% of persons with a severe Major Depressive Disorder die by suicide.

Major Depressive Disorder is like periodically falling into a hole.

2. Dysthymic Disorder — Chronically Depressed Most of the Time

Dysthymic Disorder is the hardest type of depression to recognise as it presents itself as one long period of feeling low and sufferers come to accept the constant down feelings as part of everyday life. Though the depression is not as severe as in Major Depressive Disorder, it is nonetheless debilitating and hinders sufferers from reaching their full potential in life.

To be diagnosed as having Dysthymic Disorder, sufferers must be chronically depressed for **most of the day, most days each week, for at least two years** in adults and one year in adolescents and children, and experience at least two (2) of the following symptoms:

- Poor appetite or overeating
- Insomnia or hypersomnia
- Low energy or fatigue
- Low self-esteem
- Poor concentration
- Difficulty making decisions
- Feelings of hopelessness.

The features of Dysthymic Disorder are similar to those of a Major Depressive Episode. However, in Major Depressive Disorder, there exist discrete episodes (depressive episode and recovery), whereas in Dysthymic Disorder, mood change is less severe but continuous. It is like always walking knee-deep in the mud. The going is hard work and tiresome.

People suffering from Dysthymic Disorder often note a change in feelings. They feel sad for no reason or have 'slowed down' and feel tired all the time. There are also changes in their behaviour, for example, excessive crying because of their chronic sadness, outbursts of anger and/or loss of sexual desire. They brood, complain and sleep badly. Although they feel they are inadequate they usually cope with the basic demands of everyday life. Dysthymic Disorder is characterised by its consistency and the symptoms can last for months, years, sometimes indefinately. Not all of the symptoms must be present to suffer from Dysthymic Disorder.

Sufferers are often not aware that something is wrong as the onset of this type of depression can be relatively early, in childhood, adolescence, or at the latest, early adulthood. When the onset is later in life, the disorder often occurs in the aftermath of a discrete depressive episode and is associated with bereavement or other obvious stress.

Because the symptoms have often been present for many years, they seem to be second nature. Therefore, it can be difficult to distinguish from the normal behaviour or moods and the depressive symptoms of the person. In most cases, sufferers don't know that they could be feeling much better. They consider the symptoms of the disorder as part of normal life and often speak of 'having always felt this way'. Frequently, Dysthymic Disorder is only diagnosed when the sufferer seeks help for another problem.

NEED PROFESSIONAL HELP?

There are a number of physical conditions that can cause symptoms similar to dysthymia. Consult with your physician to determine if your symptoms are not based on a physical ailment. Despite the long-term nature of this type of depression, psychotherapy is effective in reducing the symptoms of depression and assisting the person in managing his/her life better. Some individuals with Dysthymic Disorder respond well to antidepressant medication.

Dysthymic Disorder is like constantly walking through mud, the going is hard work.

23

3. Bipolar Disorder — Swinging From One Extreme to the Other

Although Bipolar Disorder, also known as Manic-Depressive illness, is probably the most widely known type of depression, it is often misunderstood. Bipolar causes unusual shifts in a person's mood, their energy and their ability to function. Unlike the usual ups and downs we all experience in life, the symptoms of Bipolar Disorder are much more intensified. This elevation of mood can be euphoric (feeling happier than usual) or it can be experienced as an extreme irritability, impulsivity, anger and/or aggression. This aspect of the illness is called a manic episode if the elevated, expansive or irritable mood lasts for at least seven days. If it lasts only four days, or if it is less severe, it is termed a hypomanic episode.

Manic Episode

The DSM-IV-TR states that a manic episode has elevated mood for at least one (1) week and is accompanied by three (3) of the following additional symptoms of the disorder.

- Inflated self-esteem or grandiosity, an 'I can do anything'-attitude
- Decreased need for sleep, feeling rested after only a couple of hours of sleep
- Excessive talking, deep need to communicate, will start intimate conversations with strangers
- Flights of fancy, unrealistic and often impossible ideas and beliefs
- Easily distracted by unimportant things, short attention span
- Increased involvement in goal related activities, becoming obsessed in doing something
- Psychomotor (physical) agitation, hyperactive,reslessness, can't sit still, pacing, nervous gestures

During a manic episode, the sufferer is in an elevated, expansive mood. Extreme cheerfulness, on a constant high and a 'nothing is impossible' state of mind also accompanies the manic episodes. In their unwarranted optimism and grandiosity, sufferers often show a provocative, intrusive, or aggressive behaviour. Their uncritical self-confidence can result in poor judgment, which can lead to risky and foolish business ventures, reckless driving, buying sprees drug, alcohol abuse and sexual promiscuity. The consequences of their actions can often be costly, if not dangerous. They may sometimes find themselves engaging with people who may take advantage of them, or get caught up in questionable or controversial circumstances. Warnings from family and friends to slow down are often rejected. On the contrary, if they encounter resistance, or their actions or wishes are being thwarted, they easily become irritable. There is no consistency in their moods and they frequently alternate between euphoria and irritability.

Mild manic episodes may even feel good to the person who experiences it and can result in good functioning and enhanced productivity. Some may become highly creative with innovative ideas popping easily into their minds. Obstacles don't seem to exist and reality checks are pushed aside. They think faster and may even begin to talk faster, but do have a tendency to jump from one subject to the next. Even though family and friends recognise the mood swings as possible bipolar behaviour, the person may deny that anything is wrong. There is a high probability that projects and adventures started during a manic episode fail as they can seldom be followed through because the depressive episode is usually just around the corner.

*When suffering Bipolar Disorder you may
be on top of the world one week....*

Depressive Episode

According to the DSM-IV-TR a depressive episode in Bipolar Disorder is diagnosed if five (5) or more of the depressive symptoms last most of the day, nearly every day for a period of two weeks or longer. The signs and symptoms of a depressive episode include:

- Lasting sad, anxious, or empty mood
- Feelings of hopelessness or pessimism
- Feelings of guilt, worthlessness, or helplessness
- Loss of interest or pleasure in activities once enjoyed, including sex
- Decreased energy, a feeling of fatigue or of being "slowed down"
- Difficulty concentrating, remembering, making decisions
- Restlessness or irritability
- Difficulty in accepting even minor criticisms
- Sleeping too much, or can't sleep
- Change in appetite and/or unintended weight loss or gain
- Chronic pain or other persistent bodily symptoms that are not caused by physical illness or injury
- Thoughts of death or suicide, or suicide attempts

Sometimes, severe depressive episodes can include psychotic symptoms such as hallucinations (hearing, seeing, or otherwise sensing the presence of things not actually there) and delusions. For example, the sufferer may believe he or she is ruined, or their presence has a detrimental effect on others, or they have committed some terrible crime. They may feel responsible for negative events that happen to family and friends or society at large.

Some may also experience episodes of paranoia where they feel that everyone has turned against them or they may feel they are being singled out and persecuted. Believing that everybody is out to get them, sufferers may become defensive and aggressive without provocation. These strong emotional responses tend to reflect the extreme state of mind at the time.

There is also the possibility that sufferers of Bipolar Disorder experience mixed episodes. A mixed episode is when they have both manic and major depressive symptoms nearly every day for at least one week. Their mood varies with the time of the day and they can go from a high in the morning to a deep low in the afternoon or vice versa. This is not only debilitating and confusing for the sufferer but also for those around him or her.

Sufferers of Bipolar Disorder do not exclusively alternate between extreme highs and extreme lows. They can experience normal periods as well. Like other mental disorders, there is no physiological test that can identify Bipolar Disorder. The diagnosis is made on the basis of symptoms, the course of the illness and family history. Anxiety disorders often accompany Bipolar Disorder.

NEED PROFESSIONAL HELP?

It is definitely advised to seek professional help. Without proper treatment manic and/or depressive episodes can become quite severe and out of control. If the symptoms of Bipolar Disorder are left untreated they can have a profound impact on the sufferer, family and friends and it could lead to marriage, family and financial problems. There is a tendency to self-harm. Medication for Bipolar has proven to be very effective in managing the symptoms in most sufferers.

...and down in the dumps the next week.

4. Cyclothymic Disorder — Constant Up and Down

Cyclothymic Disorder is probably the least disruptive of the depressive disorders in everyday life. It is characterised by numerous bouts of elevated, expansive or irritable mood, consistent with hypomania, and depressive symptoms. People who have Cyclothymic Disorder go through periods of being mildly depressed followed by highs where they feel great. The changes can be sudden, sometimes only lasting a few hours, days or weeks. The mood swings are usually perceived by the sufferer as being unrelated to life events. Without prolonged observation and a good account of the sufferer's previous behaviour, this disorder is difficult to diagnose. Because the mood swings are relatively mild and the periods of mood elevation may be enjoyable, cyclothymia frequently fails to come to medical attention.

This fluctuation of moods must last for at least two (2) years with no more than two months of "normal" moods interrupting the cycle. For children and adolescents, the duration must be at least one (1) year. Although they are very similar, the hypomanic symptoms of Cyclothymic Disorder are less pronounced than the manic symptoms of the Bipolar Disorder and are usually fewer in number.

Hypomanic Symptoms: (as listed in the DSM-IV-TR)

-   Inflated self-confidence, I can do everything better than others

-   Decreased need for sleep, feels rested after three hours of sleep

-   More talkative, pressure to keep talking and express their opinion

-   Flight of ideas, thoughts racing through the mind at 100 mph

-   Easily distracted by unimportant things, constantly switches focus

-   Physical agitation, hyperactive, pacing, shaking

-   Increase in goal-directed activities,sometimes obsessive in pursuing a goal

-   Excessive involvement in pleasurable activities, such as buying sprees, sexual indiscretions.

-   Marked change in mood and functioning, which is noted by others.

Depressive Symptoms:
- Lack of attention to daily responsibilities
- Feeling hopeless or guilty
- Bouts of crying
- Inability to make decisions
- Changes in sleep patterns
- Uninterested in life and things that used to be enjoyed

The hypomanic and depressive symptoms of Cyclothymic Disorder are not severe enough to cause serious impairment of social or occupational functioning and usually do not require hospitalisation. There are no psychotic components in the disorder. The change in functioning may only be noticeable by an obvious increase in efficiency, accomplishments and creativity. However, in some people, the suddenness of the mood swings can create some disruption in their social and working environment.

NEED PROFESSIONAL HELP?

If this description matches your mood swings it is advisable to talk to your doctor. If left untreated there is a reasonable probability that Cyclothymic Disorder can develop into Bipolar Disorder. Cyclothymic Disorder can be successfully treated through a combination of medication and therapy.

Inflated self-confidence is a marked symptom of Cyclothymic Disorder.

Depression is something we are able to deal with relatively well. The scientific knowledge of treating depression can be compared, for example, with the knowledge of treating Aids or cancer. There is much more known about treating depression than there is about treating Aids or cancer. Medication and psychotherapies, such as Cognitive Behaviour Therapy, have shown to be helpful in managing depression.

* * *

Symptoms of Depression

Now that we know the different types of depression, let's have a look at the symptoms of the most common disorder: The Major Depressive Disorder. It is normal to occasionally feel low and off balance, sad or even sorry for oneself. Usually such a feeling passes within a few days and we bounce back to our normal outlook on life. The difference between feeling down and actually suffering from depression is in the intensity of the symptoms, how long they last and the degree to which they impact on our life. To be classified as a symptom of depression changes must be noticed in either the sufferer's

moods (i.e. feeling depressed, worthless);

or **behaviour** (i.e. social withdrawal, irritation);

in his or her **functions** (i.e. problems in thinking, loss of concentration);

or **physical attributes** (i.e. insomnia or hypersomnia, weight changes).

According to the DSM-IV-TR, we need to be in a depressed mood every day for at least two consecutive weeks to be diagnosed as experiencing a depressive episode. The depressive episode hinders us in our social and/or family life, as well as at our place of work and other important areas of our life. Sufferers can lose the energy to even take care of themselves, and in extreme cases, it can lead to suicide.

When depressed you sometimes dig yourself deeper into the depression hole.

If the major depressive episode is of a milder nature then we may still be able to perform our duties at work and at home satisfactorily, but it may take a lot more effort to do so. Some people going through a depressive episode like this describe it as feeling "down in the dumps".

It takes time to understand depression and to get some control over it. Depression is indiscriminate, it doesn't pick and choose certain types of people to attack and it can happen to anyone. Depression appears on all social levels and it affects not only the sufferer, but also those close to him or her. It is therefore not surprising that depression often runs in families from one generation to the next. Scientists are still arguing if depression is heredity, or if it is caused through upbringing or environmental circumstances. Most likely, depression occurs because of all of these factors. Even if someone does have a genetic predisposition towards depression, it is usually a stressful, or unhappy life event or events that triggers the onset of a depressive episode.

In a society, which celebrates the 'can-do' attitude and thrives on achievement, people who suffer from depression can find themselves increasingly out–of-step. Depression is not something we can just 'snap out of' if we would only try. Society's push for people to 'pull themselves together and get on with it' alienates sufferers more from their surroundings and they retreat even further, sometimes into total isolation, thereby digging themselves deeper into the depression hole. There are countless people silently suffering from depression, not seeking help because of the fear they will be ridiculed, or ostracised.

In order to be able to manage depression and get control of our life, it is vital to understand the different aspects of depression. The DSM-IV-TR states that a Major Depressive Episode must be accompanied by at least four (4) of the symptoms described hereafter.

WARNING: If you have experienced any of these symptoms or they 'ring true' to you it is best to seek professional guidance and assistance. We should refrain from diagnosing ourselves as similar symptoms may sometimes have other underlying causes.

a) Continually Feeling Low

The most classic symptom of a major depressive episode is a very low mood, persisting over a longer period of time. This can present itself as a deep sadness or a feeling of emptiness. The sufferer is easily discouraged and sees no point in making an effort. A sense of hopelessness can also be present. Some become tearful for no apparent reason. Others experience this low feeling as having no feelings at all. They claim that nothing really touches them and they often speak that they feel "blasé" and disinterested about everything. However, their facial expressions, general attitude and behaviour show all the hallmarks of suffering from depression.

Sadness and hopelessness can also transform into anger and increased irritability. Some sufferers may respond to trivial matters and events with angry outbursts and exaggerated frustration. It often seems that the depressed person is constantly 'jumping down someone's throat'. They are quick to blame others for their annoyances. Children and adolescents in particular are more prone to become irritable and cranky. Men are also more likely to express irritability and anger rather than admitting that they are feeling low, and they are less prepared to talk about their moods or their emotions. This makes it harder for health professionals to diagnose depression in men, which in turn is often left untreated and can become severe and disabling.

You feel low over a longer period of time.

b) Loss of Interest and/or Pleasure

In a depressive episode, loss of interest nearly always occurs. The sufferer has reduced, or sometimes no interest, in life and their surroundings. There is a significant decrease in the amount of pleasure they find in activities, which they once enjoyed. Hobbies are no longer pursued. They may lose their enthusiasm for their favourite sport or activity. What was once fun and motivating is now seen as dull and meaningless. A general attitude of 'not caring anymore' surfaces. Men will acknowledge that they have lost interest in their hobbies or sports, but they usually put this loss of interest down to being too busy at work, getting older or just going through a phase at the moment, than it being a sign of depression.

Family members and friends are usually the first to notice that the sufferer has withdrawn from social activities. Attempts to involve the sufferer in everyday life often fail. They claim they are too tired to make an effort or just not in the mood right now. Some may even deliberately sabotage close relationships and friendships. This isolation results in a loss of social support, which in turn further increases the feelings of loneliness, isolation and depression. Many people also experience a significant decline in sexual interest, which has a negative effect on intimate relationships and the sufferer may fall deeper into depression.

You don't participate in social activities like you used to.

34

c) Sleep Disturbance: Insomnia or Hypersomnia

Our sleeping patterns tend to be particularly sensitive to changes in our moods. Emotional upset quickly translates into having difficulties sleeping. Insomnia, (not being able to sleep), is one of the most frustrating symptoms of depression. It seems that no matter how tired you are as soon as your head hits the pillow you are wide awake. You've counted herds of sheep in your mind and drank gallons of hot coco and camomile tea and just nothing seems to put you to sleep. According to DSM-IV-TR a large proportion of depressed people suffer from insomnia. This presents itself as not being able to fall asleep and/or not being able to stay asleep. The sufferer may continually wake up during the night and have difficulty returning to sleep despite extreme tiredness. A classical symptom of insomnia is early morning waking. Sometimes sleep can only be achieved with the help of medication. Insomnia can be extremely persistent and last months, even years.

Although it is less common, at the other end of the scale there is also hypersomnia. In this case, the sufferer cannot stop sleeping and generally has a prolonged nighttime sleep (i.e. they oversleep). People suffering from hypersomnia may also have increased daytime sleeps. As with insomnia, the sufferer of hypersomnia is constantly tired. Both insomnia and hypersomnia can cause loss of energy and fatigue.

You can't fall asleep and/or keep on waking up in the early hours.

d) Appetite and Weight Changes – Weight Loss

Significant change in weight is a common symptom of depression. According to DSM-IV-TR the change should be more than 5% of body weight within a month. The weight loss must not be due to dieting and/or increased exercise. Some sufferers have a dramatically reduced appetite resulting in significant weight loss. They often simply forget to eat or they develop a general indifference or maybe even an adversion to food and feel as if they have to force themselves to eat.

Depression has also been closely linked to the development of eating disorders, such as Anorexia and Bulimia, especially in adolescent females. In these cases the sufferer becomes obsessed with being thin. They believe that not being thin enough is the cause of their depression and if they can control their weight they will be able to control their depression and ultimately their life. They view food as their enemy, which must be eliminated at all costs. They will either not eat at all, or will only eat extremely small amounts. The danger is that even once they have lost a great deal of weight, they continue to think they are fat and keep trying to lose weight, even though they are emaciated. With Bulimia, sufferers will alternate between binge eating and purging. Both disorders can lead to serious health problems and in the worst-case scenario, even death.

You lose more than 5% of bodyweight within a month.

Weight Gain

On the other hand, some people gain weight when depressed within a relatively short time. The usual scenario is that of "comfort eating", where a person turns to food in times of stress and/or when their mood is down. In a small percentage of people, it can even lead to overeating or binge eating. It is therefore not surprising that being obese, or overweight, is often associated with having depression. Psychological studies have established that eating does temporarily reduce the stress of negative feelings. Unfortunately, the relief does not last very long and is usually followed by feelings of guilt, sometimes even shame and disgust.

Despite numerous resolutions to stick to a strict diet and exercise, depressed people find it difficult to follow through. They often seek specific foods, such as sweets or carbohydrates, which raise blood sugar levels and give an instant emotional lift. However, this lasts only for a short period of time. Afterwards, the sugar levels drop and they start feeling low and hungry again. The inevitable weight gain causes the sufferer to sink further into a depression. It can be a vicious cycle. Sufferers are depressed because they are overweight and they are overweight because they are depressed. If you have gained considerable weight within a short time check with your doctor first, to make sure this is not caused by an underlying health problem.

You gain more than 5% of body weight within a month.

e) Agitation or Physical Restlessness

Markedly increased irritation and agitation is another symptom of a major depressive episode. Sufferers have a tendency to overreact to minor annoyances. They easily lose their composure and have angry outbursts for the slightest of reasons and often without any provocation. Their frustration levels are very high and their tolerance very low. They show signs of inflexibility and can become rigid in opinions and behaviour.

On the physical side, people suffering from this symptom often display an increased restlessness. They find it difficult to sit still. Their hands, arms, legs or whole bodies, may start shaking, or they may begin pacing. Wringing of the hands and rubbing skin or clothing can be another sign. However, if your legs start shaking, particularly when you rest and later in the day, it might be worthwhile to see your doctor. You may have Restless Leg Syndrom.

Collectively, these types of activities are known as psychomotor agitation. Sufferers may also experience a slowing down of speech, thinking and body movements. These symptoms are described as psychomotor retardation. If unusual tremor symptoms start to appear it is best to seek medical advice to make sure there is no other medical cause responsible for the shakes and tremors.

You easily get irritated and agitated and may even start shaking.

f) Fatigue, Loss of Energy

A very common sign of depression is a profound loss of energy, often combined with a persistent fatigue. The smallest tasks require a substantial effort and sufferers often stay at home and avoid social interaction. Not having enough stamina to get up and go to work or fulfill one's obligations can have profound social and economical consequences not only for the sufferer but for their family as well. This can result in difficulties in personal and working relationships and financial hardship.

Sufferers often take on an attitude of apathy or 'what's the point in trying' and in more serious cases people will start to neglect even the most basic tasks, such as cooking, cleaning, shopping and personal hygiene. People suffering from this depressive symptom have been known to live in the same pair of pyjamas for weeks. In milder forms of this symptom, sufferers become less efficient in their work and fail to finish projects. Simple things suddenly take twice as long to perform and more mistakes are made.

On the physical side, loss of energy translates into lack of activity, which in turn results in loss of muscle tone, muscle mass and bone mass. These effects can lead to degeneration in physique, strength, physical well-being, and may lead to the person becoming overweight.

You are constantly tired and have no energy.

g) Feelings of Worthlessness or Guilt

A low sense of self worth usually accompanies a major depressive episode. Sufferers are prone to putting themselves down at every opportunity. They feel they are not good at anything or important to anyone. They find it hard to accept compliments or will devalue their achievements. They end up setting their personal benchmark higher and higher, thus making it impossible to meet expectations. They will also interpret minor everyday upsets as personal defects and failings. In a sense they become their own worst enemy. Low self worth can also manifest itself physically. The sufferer may have a bad body posture, slumped shoulders and walk hunched over. Their facial expressions may show despair and a deep sadness.

Sufferers can also experience intense feelings of guilt and often start to blame themselves for other people's behaviour and transgressions. If something is wrong in their family life or if their spouse is unfaithful they blame themselves. If their friends treat them badly they feel it is somehow their fault. They may even accept responsibility for events outside of their control. This can reach delusional proportions, where sufferers may feel responsible for things such as bad weather, natural catastrophes, or the state of the economy. Low self-esteem intensifies depression and the sufferer's view of the world becomes increasingly negative which can result in a general apathy.

You feel you are not worth very much or feel guilty for everything.

h) Loss of Concentration

Depression can seriously impair the sufferer's ability to concentrate. Not being able to think straight is a very annoying symptom of a major depressive episode. Any attention span can shrink down to zero and as soon as information is received, it is already forgotten. Sufferers set out to do something and within seconds they forget what it was. It seems impossible to keep their mind focused on the task at hand and they are blown off course by the slightest interruption. In addition they seem to be constantly looking for things and find it difficult to organise their life.

This same symptom also effects the decision making process. Sufferers have a diminished ability to assess and judge everyday situations. Somehow they cannot grasp the facts of a situation and don't know which way to turn. This in turns leads to general confusion about their life, their options and the future. Every path seems to be the wrong one. Consequently they feel paralysed and either take no action at all or they make impulsive panic driven decisions, which are mostly destined to fail. Some may want that someone else takes over the responsibility for their life and makes the decisions for them. Or they may let things slide until a decision is forced upon them by circumstances. Needless to say this is never the best option and decisions achieved this way are hardly ever in their best interest.

You are often confused and have difficulties making decisions.

i) Recurrent Dark Thoughts

Thoughts of suicide and death are one of the most dangerous symptoms of severe depression. These dark thoughts invade every part of the sufferer's life. The joy of living, meeting challenges and setting personal goals all seems to be futile. Sufferers often toy with the idea of planning their suicide and spend much time imagining the effect this drastic step would have on their surroundings. The thought that others would be better off if the sufferer was dead is often prevalent and leads to suicide attempts or in the worst case, a completed suicide. In Australia the suicide rate is four times higher in men than it is in women because men are less likely to seek help when depressed.

Less severely affected individuals may intermittently dwell on committing suicide for short periods of time. In extreme cases, sufferers may have already made preparations to commit suicide by obtaining the means and selecting a location and time. Suicide is often motivated by feelings of hopelessness and by the desire to end their own suffering, as well as the perceived suffering of their loved ones.

If you, or someone else, are thinking about suicide call your general practitioner, or the emergency helpline, or go to your local hospital's emergency room. Try not to be alone when you are in this emotional state. Similarly, don't leave anybody alone who is suicidal.

You often think about suicide or harming yourself.

Medication - Pills are Not Just Pills

The previous chapters have informed us about what depression is and how it manifests itself. Now we will investigate what options we have to start managing the problem effectively. Your doctor may suggest medication as part of your initial or ongoing treatment plan. However, many of us are tempted to reject medication from the start because of misinformation and the stigma attached to taking antidepressant medication. So how can medication help with our depression?

Medication plays an important role in the treatment of depression and depressive disorders. It gives acute symptomatic relief and longer-term protection against relapse. In the majority of cases medication is helpful, but outcomes are consistently better when psychological treatments, in particular Cognitive Behaviour Therapy, are used as well. Antidepressants are prescription drugs and should only be taken under the supervision of a doctor.

Antidepressants are not happy pills that make us euphoric or lose our inhibitions and equally, they don't turn us into zombies either. Taking antidepressants to help manage depression is not a sign of personal weakness, or something to be ashamed of. Whether medication is the best treatment option depends on how severe the depression is, the history of the depression and the age of the sufferer. There is good evidence that antidepressants are highly effective with severe depression in adults, often combined with psychotherapy.

Unfortunately, all medications have side effects, as well as benefits. Your prescribing physician's main task is to find the right balance between controlling the symptoms and minimising the associated side effects. Your doctor should provide you with information about the possible side effects you can expect and how long these may last. Sometimes certain side effects, such as dizziness or nausea, only last until the body gets used to the medication. It usually takes at least a couple of weeks until the antidepressants work to their full capacity. If it takes longer for you to feel the effects, or if you experience side effects other than what your doctor informed you about, contact your doctor. If your doctor decides to switch you to a different drug, they will phase out one drug over the course of a couple of weeks, before starting the next. Do not stop taking your medication without your doctor's consent.

There are many different types of antidepressant medications. They differ in terms of their effectiveness against different depressive features, and in terms of their side-effect profiles. The main groups of antidepressants used today are the tricyclic antidepressants and the selective serotonin re-uptake inhibitors (SSRI's). Newer types of antidepressants are also becoming available and their efficiency in treatment is very encouraging.

The scientific literature seems to suggest that antidepressants can also be used to treat people with different psychiatric problems. Some of them are:

- Moderate to severe depression (Not mild depression).

- Severe anxiety and panic attacks

- Obsessive compulsive disorders

- Chronic pain

- Eating disorders

- Post-traumatic Stress Disorder

The MAOI Group

The monoamine oxidase inhibitors (MAOI's) were one of the first really effective antidepressants on the market. The three neurotransmitters, (serotonin, norepinephrine, and dopamine) are known as monoamines and are responsible for transmitting messages in the brain. Once they have done their job, they get burned up by a protein in the brain called monoamine oxidase, a liver and brain enzyme. The MAOI group of antidepressants work by blocking this cleanup activity. Therefore, the excess neurotransmitters don't get destroyed but start building up in the brain, which in turn makes the patient feel better.But there is a problem in this process and this group of antidepressants has some serious safety concerns associated with it, such as intolerance to certain foods and blood pressure problems, which must be considered. The enzyme monoamine oxidase also mops up a molecule called tyramine, which affects blood pressure. One of the things that the MAOI drugs also do is block the burning up of tyramine and this can cause a sudden, sometimes even fatal, increase in blood pressure. Certain foods contain tyramine and therefore it is necessary to follow a strict diet when taking any drugs of the MAOI group.

Safety Warning: It is imperative that you inform doctors and dentists that you are taking MAOI's before any surgery, or emergency treatment – even if you stopped taking the drug up to two weeks ago. The anesthesia combined with MAOI's can cause a drop in blood pressure. You may want to carry an ID card noting that you are taking this medicine.

The Tricyclic Group

Another one of the longstanding groups of antidepressants are the tricyclics, also known as TCA's. Until recently, these drugs were considered the first line of defense in the battle against depression and have been so since the late 1950's. Today, TCA's are prescribed less frequently than the new generation of antidepressants, but are still an important weapon in the antidepressant arsenal, particularly for people who don't respond well to other treatment options.

Tricyclics work against depression by stopping, or slowing down, the absorption of chemicals in the brain called noradrenaline and serotonin. These chemicals are involved in the transmission of signals down the nerves in the brain. The concentration of these neurotransmitters builds up and improves communication between certain nerve cells or neurons, which in turn lifts our mood.

Like all antidepressants, the tricyclics should be tapered off only under the care of a physician. The tricyclics have more side effects associated with them than the newer SSRI's, such as increased or irregular heart beat. It is important that your doctor carefully monitors you when taking them, especially if you have a history of serious heart disease. Your physician will have discussed these side effects with you. If you have other physical health problems, or any concerns regarding the side effects, it should be brought to the attention of your doctor as soon as possible.

The SSRI Group

The new generation of antidepressants, known as the SSRI's (selective serotonin re-uptake inhibitors), are the most utilised antidepressants today. Their main benefit is that they treat depression with less adverse effects than the TCA group or MAOI's. The SSRI group regulates the neurochemical serotonin, which is known as the feel-good chemical. By selectively inhibiting the re-uptake of serotonin, the level starts to build up, thus making us feel better.

Although the SSRI's have been praised as the wonder drugs against depression, it is important to note that there are still side effects. However, these are usually mild, not permanent and manageable.

Possible side effects include:

- Anxiety or nervousness
- Gastrointestinal distress (nausea and diarrhea)
- Headache
- Insomnia
- Tremor, dizziness
- Skin effects or rash
- Slight weight loss
- Erectile difficulty in men
- Lose of interest in sex for both men and women and a reduced ability to achieve orgasm

Frequently asked Questions about Antidepressants:

Are antidepressants addictive?

All drugs have the potential to be addictive. However, antidepressants have shown to have very low potential for addiction.

Will the antidepressants change my personality?

Antidepressants allow you to work toward positive changes in your mood state and thinking patterns and help you to experience the full range of human emotions without feeling overwhelmed. It is highly unlikely to change your personality.

How long will I have to take a medication?

There is no absolute answer to this question. You and your doctor will decide on how long you need to take your medication. You need to ask your doctor to review your medication regularly, i.e. about every six months. While it often is tempting to stop taking the medication when you feel better, do not stop because it is not helpful. It is important to continue until you and your doctor agree that the time is ripe for you to stop taking it. Remember, you and your doctor must come to this decision jointly.

* * *

Cognitive Behaviour Therapy (CBT)

Learning to manage depression through therapy has shown encouraging results. This can either be done in conjunction with medication or on its own. There are many different types of psychotherapies available today, but the most commonly used and the most promising in recent years is Cognitive Behaviour Therapy (CBT). This is a therapy that is easy to understand and user friendly.

CBT is a combination of two highly effective psychotherapies, cognitive therapy and behaviour therapy. The cognitive part is all about learning to think differently. It teaches us to recognise how certain thinking patterns can give us a distorted picture of the happenings in our life. This can result in us misconstruing situations and subsequently feeling anxious, depressed or angry, unnecessarily.

A distorted view of events may even entice us to take actions that are not in our best interest, which brings us to the behaviour part of the therapy. It shows us that we can react differently to certain events and situations in our life. Understanding the distortions helps us to weaken and eventually cut the emotional connections between disturbing events and our habitual reaction to them. It teaches us how to act and do things differently so that we can lead a happier and more fulfilling life. Put simply, we can learn to behave our way to success.

CBT encourages us to assess our surroundings from other angles. In addition to our negative view of things, the aim of CBT is to get us to look at situations from positive and/or neutral positions. This gives us a more balanced picture and we can thereby make more informative choices. Learning to apply CBT in daily life is a bit like learning to ride a bicycle, a bit wobbly at first, but once we get the hang of it, it becomes second nature.

In CBT, and preferably under the guidance of a mental health professional, we are asked to re-examine our beliefs, thoughts and values and to assess if these are still applicable. We learn to look at our problems from a new perspective. The ultimate goal is to help us lead a better life by reclaiming power and reducing the influence the past, outside events and other people's perceptions have over us.

CBT helps to pinpoint problems and identify which thoughts and behaviours need to be changed. CBT gives a clear structure to therapy and remains focused on the treatment goal. It is a very active therapy and requires a hands-on approach from all participants. Although CBT does explore past experiences and events, its main aim is to bring about improvement in our feelings and moods. Therefore, CBT concentrates on the present and is more forward-looking than other traditional therapies.

CBT is a clinically proven breakthrough in the treatment for depression and has helped countless people suffering from a variety of mental disorders and mental health problems to improve their lives. CBT has become the preferred therapy for:

- Depression and Mood Disorders
- Anxiety Disorders
- Panic Attacks and Phobias
- Obsessive-Compulsive Disorders
- Post Traumatic Stress Disorder
- Eating Disorders

It is also the preferred therapy for many other disorders and physical illnesses, such as pain.

Most mental health professionals are familiar with CBT and many specialise in this form of therapy. If you would like to undergo CBT with a professional, your family physician would certainly be able to refer you to a therapist. Otherwise, councils or state government departments for mental health or hospitals will definitely have a list of qualified professionals.

CBT addresses our emotions, our cognitions (thought processes) and our thoughts (actual contents of our thoughts). Therefore it is important to understand what each of these three components are and how they interrelate to one another.

How are Emotions Made?

Let us first look at our emotions. What are they? What do they consist of and how are they made? Emotions are an integral part of every person's life. Nothing is more important to the quality and purpose of our being than emotions. They make life worth living. Emotions have a wide-ranging and long-lasting effect on our mental and physical wellbeing. Our whole inner life consists of emotions. With the help of emotions, we gain self-knowledge and are able to measure our surroundings and our role in society better. Primitive people relied on emotions to assess danger, using them to identify when it was time to flee a situation, or time to attack. Being able to feel and create emotions is one of our most useful tools.

Emotions are created through our interpretation of events and situations around us and the events that befall us. Any outside stimuli leads us to assess and interpret the event based on our own experiences and then we make a choice, either consciously or subconsciously, as to how we will feel and subsequently react to the event. We may choose to feel positive about an event and react positively or neutrally. Or we may choose to feel negative and react negatively. Through this process we create emotions. Virtually everything we see, hear, witness or experience, generates some level of emotional response in us, which in turn will influence our actions. We all experience, or produce, dozens of emotions every day.

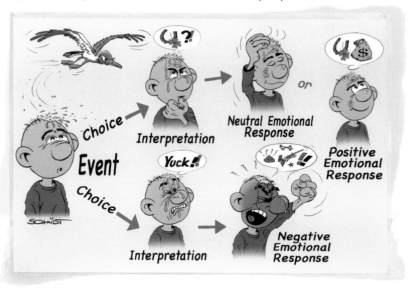

51

What are Cognitions?

The second component, which is addressed in CBT, is our cognitions. What are cognitions exactly and how do they relate to our emotions and our thoughts? Cognitions are the thought processes that go on in our mind and these are based on our personal value system, or our "rule book", which we have established during our lifetime.

If two people witness exactly the same event, will they feel exactly the same emotions? The answer is no. Why? Because each of us see any event through our own unique set of glasses. We interpret everything that happens in our lives according to our own rules, in other words, according to our own cognitions. One person who has experienced positive feelings in the past about a similar event may see the positive side of a situation and feel positive, which provides emotional strength. Another person who has had a negative emotional experience may focus on the negative, which can sap their emotional energy.

This value system is influenced by everything we were taught as children by our parents, our teachers and people who had some influence on our lives, as well as by our religion, our culture and our ethnic background. It has also been formed by what has worked for us in the past to achieve a goal, and what has not. Put differently, our cognitions are influenced

Sometimes our glasses through which we view the world have cracks.

by our own successes and failures and the conclusions that we have reached from these experiences. For example, if a child puts on a tantrum in a store and the mother gives the child a chocolate to calm down, then the child will learn that tantrums have a positive effect - it gets chocolate. Therefore, the child will be using the 'tantrum' behaviour in the future to get things it wants. If it keeps on getting what it wants, throwing a tantrum may become a lifelong habit and become part of its value system.

We begin compiling our value system, or cognitions, the moment we are born and we add to it constantly. This system determines what we feel in any given situation, what we say and what we do. The problem is that some of these rules have passed their use-by date. The circumstances to which they applied once may no longer exist and instead of being useful, they have become more of a hindrance. Coming back to our example of throwing tantrums. As adults this behaviour isn't going to win us any friends. On the contrary, we might get rejected because of it. The same behaviour that once achieved a positive reaction now achieves a negative one. It's only natural that we become confused.

That is what CBT is all about: re-examining old values and rules and if they no longer apply or are beneficial, throwing them out or replacing them with new ones.

With CBT we can learn how to replace old thinking patterns with new ones.

Automatic Thoughts

Nothing has more influence on our emotional life than our thoughts and CBT uses our thoughts to bring about positive change in our life with the aim of ultimately defeating depression. As mentioned, everything that goes on in our mind is filtered through our very own set of rules, our cognitions, which we have acquired over the course of our lives. This also applies to our thoughts, which in turn largely determine the way we feel and how we act or react. So the solution to all our emotional problems would be: if we think or process information positively, we will feel positive. In theory that may seem like all it takes, but in reality, it is not that simple.

If we were mainly told as a child that we couldn't do anything right, it is only logical that we grow up believing we are incapable of doing things and we will hesitate to challenge ourselves. Actually we will think "I can't do it!" and really believe it. The thought "I can't do that" is going to keep on popping into our head every time we want to try something new. This is called an automatic thought. Automatic thoughts appear with lightning speed and are the bridge between events and emotions. To make matters even worse, it is usually not just one negative automatic thought that makes its presence felt, but a whole string of them. Most of the time we don't realize they are flooding our mind with negative information.

One negative automatic thought leads to another and to the next and so forth. The thought:

> "I can't do it" may lead to…
> "I'm dumb" which may be followed by…
> "I'll never achieve anything" and…
> "I won't find a job" to …
> "I won't be able to support a family" to…
> "I'll be lonely and unloved" and finally to…
> "My life is a failure".

This downward spiral of negative automatic thoughts can keep on going until we see ourselves as a hopeless case and we assume failure before we even start a project. We will only change our opinion of ourselves when we make an effort to put the theory *"I can't do it"* or *"I'm dumb"* to the test and in the process we will most likely discover that we are quite capable and intelligent after all.

Now if our automatic thoughts are positive and we keep on telling ourselves that we are smart, good looking and successful, then there won't be a problem. Unfortunately when we are down and depressed our automatic thoughts tend to focus on the negative. These negative thoughts assume the worst about what other people think about our work and us. Negative automatic thoughts are dysfunctional and very hard to get rid of. Over the years they have worn a deep groove into our thinking and usually slip, without warning, into our consciousness, where they tend to stay until we make a concerted effort to stop these thoughts pushing us further into depression.

We have to start filling up those grooves so that we don't continue to run down the same worn negative tracks. By levelling out the ruts we can move to the left, to the right or in a different direction and liberate ourselves. Thinking differently may be difficult to begin with and falling back into old patterns seems automatic and can sometimes be downright disheartening. But if we can become aware of how we talk to ourselves and identify the negative beliefs we have held onto for many years, then we can start to change. It takes time to learn these new skills. This new way of thinking has to be practiced again and again, until we see the value in our life and ourselves.

Negative automatic thoughts can flood our mind in a flash and without warning.

55

The Cognitive Triad — Depressive Thinking

How do we actually think and how do we see our life when depressed? It has long been recognised that depressed people think differently than non-depressed people. They view themselves (Self), their environment (World) and their future (Future), more pessimistically. Professionals call this "depressive thinking" and it is represented by the Cognitive Triad, which is a form of automatic thought.

The Cognitive Triad symbolises the negative cycle we are caught up in when depressed. Positive situations, such as the boss praising our work, are ignored, belittled or distorted. Seeing one's future as bleak and hopeless only exacerbates the feeling of personal failure. Research has consistently shown that pessimistic thinking hinders us and weakens our motivation thereby increasing the possibility of failure. On the other hand, optimistic thinking boosts our morale and leads to successful performance. To break out of this cycle, the negative thinking patterns need to be turned around.

SELF
We think there is something wrong with us that makes self-acceptence and happiness impossible:
'I am a failure'

WORLD
Because of this personal inadequacy, we take more notice of negative circumstances:
'I am an outcast and my world is a bad place'

FUTURE
Which leads to a dim view of our future:
'I will never achieve anything and I will become destitute'

The Cognitive Distortions of Our Thoughts

Before we can start changing things we first need to identify what kind of thoughts go through our mind and why these are not working for us? As we have discovered, thoughts create feelings and feelings lead to actions. Therefore, the three components, thoughts, feelings and actions, are closely linked together. But when we are depressed, those cracks in the lenses of our glasses, or filters, we use to look at the world pull and twist reality in a negative way. In other words, our thoughts and feelings are distorted (i.e., cognitive distortions) and this makes life very arduous.

As the name suggests, a cognitive distortion gives us a distorted, or warped, picture of what is happening around us and makes us perceive our surroundings as more hostile than they actually are. Cognitive distortions are seldom based on actual facts, but more on false presumptions that have most likely originated some time in our past. To make things just a bit more complicated, we have a tendency to not just use one cognitive distortion, but several at the same time. We may highlight our shortcomings while refusing to acknowledge our positive points, such as being a good parent or skilled at our work. Our thoughts are focused on our liabilities rather than on our assets. Therefore to manage our depression we must identify the type of distortions that are prevalent in our thinking patterns.

When depressed we sometimes pull the picture of reality in different directions

All or Nothing / Black or White Thinking – "You are Either for Me or Against Me"

When we are depressed we sometimes have a tendency to look at everything in either black or white terms; there does not seem to be a grey area or middle ground. We can either do something perfect or we won't do it at all. 100% is the only measurement we accept. Someone is either good or bad. If a person, whom we may have perceived as being 'good', has disappointed us or doesn't live up to our expectations, then he or she will quickly be labeled as 'bad'. We find it hard to understand that a person can have positive and negative traits when black and white thinking distorts our view of reality. Another characteristic of this distortion is that we swing from hot to cold. We can be so intense until people feel suffocated, then we react by cutting all contact.

When we succumb to this distortion we tend to move from one extreme to the other and we set our expectations for our achievements, or the achievements of others, so high that there is little chance we, or others, can reach it. The inevitable disappointment depresses us even further and we often give up prematurely believing that it's no use even trying. We must learn to accept that life rarely unfolds in the extremes. Rather, life happens in the numerous possibilities between the 'all or nothing', it actually unfolds in various shades of grey and sometimes even in all the colours of the spectrum.

People and/or situations are seldom black or white.

Disqualifying the Positive — "If Things are Bad, Why Not Make Them Worse"

This is taking the 'all or nothing' thinking a step further by filtering out all the positive evidence of our performance until we are only left with the negative. Anything good is seen as nothing and can easily be explained away. Sometimes we even go as far as destroying the positive. This distortion highlights automatic thoughts that reinforce negative feelings. We perceive everything as bad and negative. For example, we might say that we have nothing positive in our lives. However, if we investigate this a bit further we discover that we have a job, a place to live, a loving family, loyal friends and much more. But, when we dismiss the positive, we might answer that the job is boring, the house needs renovating, the family costs too much and we have no time to spend with our friends. We fail to acknowledge these valuable assets and our achievements.

People who disqualify the positive have difficulty staying rational, and looking at situations from a positive, or even neutral, perspective. Negative evidence, no matter how weak, trivial or irrelevant, counts, and positive evidence, no matter how strong, is explained away. If we are caught up in this distortion, then we won't allow ourselves to feel good about anything.

When depressed we tend to destroy anything good.

Overgeneralisation — "You are All the Same!"

We have all been guilty of making an overgeneralisation at some point in our lives. When we overgeneralise, we take the outcome of an event or occurrence and conclude that things will always be the same, usually negative, when situations are similar. For example, someone from a certain ethnic background has been rude to us, now we conclude that all people from this ethnic background are rude. Or a young woman finds out her boyfriend has cheated on her. She concludes that all men are cheaters; therefore all men are untrustworthy. Her next boyfriend will have a hard time convincing her that he can be trusted.

It is needless to say that this kind of negative generalisation will taint any future contact with people from similar groups, or people encountered in similar circumstances. We will approach future relationships with some misgivings and often refuse to investigate any further if a given fact, or outcome, applies to certain individuals or circumstances. Once a fact is established in our mind, then it is seen as a certain predictor of future events. This may lead to missing out on opportunities and experiences that may enhance our lives. We are closing doors without looking what could be behind them.

*We make generalisations about people and situations
that are based on limited information or experience.*

Mental Filters — "What I Do Not Acknowledge Does Not Exist"

When we apply mental filters we only focus on one detail in any given situation, without taking into account the rest of the picture and what we do not see or know we then make up. For instance, we may be angry with our partner for coming home late. We don't question why our partner was late. We completely ignore the bigger picture; maybe he or she had a flat tyre on the way or ran out of petrol, or there was an accident on the road. They may have met an old friend and forgot the time. We label him or her unreliable and then we may make things up such as accusing them of doing something behind our backs, maybe cheating on us or that they don't care about us anymore.

There can be many reasons for things and situations to happen, things that have nothing to do with us. However, our mental filter only allows us to register that our partner wasn't there at the arranged time, therefore they deliberately let us down. They wanted to hurt us. There is no room for flexibility and taking into account the broader circumstances of the situation and we often don't give the other person the opportunity to set the record straight and explain things. It is as if we are wearing blinkers that allow us only a small field of vision and we can't see what is left or right.

We only see what we want to see and
completely ignore the rest of the picture.

Magnification — "Making Mountains Out of Molehills"

A classic distortion is magnifying the slightest mishap and turning it into the greatest personal disaster. Perfectionists are particularly prone to seeing the negative results of their actions as larger than they really are. When depressed we tend to magnify the negative, sometimes we even blow it out of proportion. This distortion often appears together with the distortion of discounting the positive.

We enlarge a small negative and refuse to acknowledge the positive of the overall picture. For example, a student who has completed an excellent essay will ignore that he or she has done a good job, but focus on one little grammatical error and enlarge it out of all proportion. The incorrect placing of a comma becomes more important than a whole chapter of clear argument. We look at our errors with a magnifying glass while completely ignoring the overall picture, which contains so many positives.

We are also prone to magnify other people's achievements and then we get depressed because our own efforts apparently can not measure up. This can paralyse us which results in us taking on no new challenges or maybe even giving up what we have been doing so far.

We pick out a minor detail of a situation and look at it through a magnifying glass and enlarge it out of all proportion.

Minimisation — "Anything Positive Does Not Count"

This is the opposite of magnification. If we are depressed we tend to either ignore, or dismiss, our own positive attributes, or the positives of a situation. For example if we are good at something, or have special skills, we label it as 'nothing, anyone can do that'. Or if a friend tells us that they like us and we look particularly good. We dismiss the positive and immediately magnify the negative by pointing out that we can be moody and dislikable and that we can't possibly look good with this nose, this haircut and those extra pounds on our hips. No outside assurances that we are attractive physically and in our personality or that we have some very valuable talents can convince us of our positives. Every compliment, or confirmation of our positive traits, is shrugged off as insignificant.

Even in the face of factual evidence, such as having made good career moves or having numerous friends who speak highly of us, we still refuse to acknowledge our professional competence, or our good social abilities and the positive influence we have on our surroundings. This is like turning the binoculars around and looking at our abilities through the wrong end. What we see is too small and too out of focus to distinguish.

By looking through the wrong end of the binoculars we can't see the positives about a situation or ourselves.

Catastrophising — "The Worst is Going to Happen or Has Happened."

Catastrophising is like stepping on a mudslide. Once we get on the slide it is extremely hard to get off again. It seems that with every disastrous assumption we gain momentum and slip further down into the emotional hole. For example, our boss points out a mistake in our work. Instead of accepting his helpful advice as something constructive we believe that we have been put on notice. In our minds eye we already see ourselves losing our job and consequently having no money and being unable to pay our bills. Debt collectors will be knocking at our door and threaten to take away our possessions. Before long we are certain that we will become bankrupt and lose our house, end up on the street and our family will be torn apart.

With every negative thought our visualisation of the possible negative events becomes worse until it reaches an extreme level. We believe our assumptions are already given facts and that we are powerless to change the chain of terrible events. We may even panic and resign from our position in the hope of gaining some control. By doing so, we unwittingly set in motion the very events we fear the most. We slide further down the mud. Thinking unhealthy thoughts leads to negative feelings, which create panic and sets in motion damaging and self-destructive behaviour.

Once we start catastrophising it is extremely hard to stop.

Jumping to Conclusions:

This distortion relates to thinking that is not based on any actual evidence, but is based on assumptions, which typically make things worse than they really are. There are three distinct forms of "Jumping to Conclusions":

a) Negative Labelling — "I'm a Loser"

Applying a negative label to other people, or an event, often entails overgeneralisation. This happens when we attribute a set of certain characteristics, which we have seen in some, to all members of a group. We often label ourselves as well. When we meet someone we tell them what we do e.g., "I am a teacher". This label tells the other person something about us. There is nothing wrong with this kind of labeling. It helps others get to know us better.

However, negative self-labeling, such as "I'm a failure", can be very damaging. The negative labels we apply to ourselves and/or others are almost always automatic thoughts. The more we use them, the more we believe them and soon they become self-fulfilling prophecies. A label is an abstraction of something. If we allow the label to become all-important, then we ignore the reality of what the label stands for.

We often label ourselves negatively.

b) Mind Reading — "I Know You Think I am Stupid"

When mind reading we think we know what other people think about us. We hear whispers behind closed doors and we immediately believe others are saying something bad about us. We think we know how they feel or judge us and this is usually negative. We become convinced they are laughing behind our backs, making fun of us and belittling us. We claim to have a sixth sense, or a powerful antenna, that will pick up all the negative vibes of others. We misread situations and other people's behaviour. When mind-reading, we automatically assume the worst about circumstances and what other people may think about us.

This belief is hardly ever based on actual facts, but rather on vague assumptions and misconceptions. Naturally this is going to alter our behaviour. For example, if we firmly believe that other people think we are stupid, then we are going to be self conscious around them and may even make more mistakes. Or if we believe they are judging us poorly, we are going to react negatively, maybe even hostile. Ultimately, we avoid other people's company and become lonely and isolated. If we would ask our friends and family what they really think about us, then we would most likely be totally surprised by how highly they regard us and our achievements.

We think we can pick up other people's thinking and opinions about us with a special antenna and receiver.

c) Fortune Telling — "I'm Going to Fail Anyway, Why Try?"

In this type of "Jumping to Conclusions" distortion we assume to know what is going to happen before it happens. We think we can look into our crystal ball and predict the negative outcome of any event. We expect failure before we start. "I know I am going to fail my driving test." This negative fortune-telling distortion can be especially damaging, as this automatic thought about a future event can easily become a self-fulfilling prophecy. We suppose that the outcome of any given situation is already predetermined and nothing we can do will change it, or have any influence over it at all.

If we believe that the outcome of a situation is already decided then we are going to perform at a far lower level than our abilities. There is no point in trying hard enough when we expect to fail. Coming back to our example of passing the driving test. Because we assume failure we are nervous and selfconscious, make silly mistakes. Sure enough, we do a bad job, thus proving we were right all along. In the fortune telling distortion we set negative goals for ourselves and then live down to them. People who are prone to using this distortion use it as an all-purpose excuse for giving up or not even attempting to achieve a goal. Most people who fail, do so because they have given up.

We think we can look into our mental crystal ball and know exactly what is going to happen, so why try to make an effort.

67

Emotional Reasoning — "Where There is Smoke, There Must be Fire"

Or "I feel it therefore it must be right." We mostly feel bad because automatic thoughts are feeding us a distorted view about a situation. With the emotional reasoning distortion we have automatic thoughts because we feel bad. Our view of a given situation is based solely on feelings. I feel bad therefore it must be bad. It is a reverse situation. Emotional reasoning amplifies the effects of other cognitive distortions.

For example we are nervous and scared before a dentist appointment. Based on our feelings, we believe that the treatment is going to be extremely painful. We start fortune telling. In fact, the dentist appointment involves a minimum of pain, but because the automatic thought said, "this is going to hurt badly", we were frightened, tense and more perceptible to pain. Or we may feel uncertain about our partner's feelings, hence we become convinced that our relationship is on the rocks and he or she wants to get rid of us. We are quarrelsome, defensive and may make unfounded accusations, subsequently our partner may leave. Because we thought we saw a bit of smoke we created a fire and brought about the very circumstances we feared. Reasoning based only on emotion will almost always make our problems worse.

We believe because we feel bad about a situation or ourselves that the situaion or we must really be bad.

'Should'-ing Yourself and Others — "I, and/or Others, Should be Perfect"

This is another version of emotional reasoning and consists of telling ourselves that we should be doing something different from what we are actually doing. We can target this distortion at ourselves and/or others. The automatic thought always entails that we "must", "should", or "ought to", do something. When 'should'-ing is applied it sometimes goes beyond logical thinking and we make impossible demands of ourselves and others. "We should've been there, then he would not have had an accident," or "we should've been more attentive, more observing or more understanding then he or she would not have left." Most likely we gave it our best shot, but things just didn't work out.

Naturally we all have obligations that we need to fulfill. There are rational explanations as to why we should do something and not other things. If we can supply a reason as to why we need to do something the "should" becomes irrelevant. "I should go shopping." Why? "Because if I don't go shopping there will be no food in the house:" compared to "We should have known he was going to hurt himself." Why? Unless he told us, how could we know what his plans were? We are not mind readers, nor are we Superman or Superwoman.

We think we, or others, should have done something different, then things would have turned out better. We expect to be better than Superman.

Personalisation and Blame — "It is Always My/Your Fault"

When we personalise we assume responsibility for things that go wrong that are outside of our control. We see it as our fault if something bad happens. The fact that the circumstances have absolutely nothing to do with us is completely ignored. For example, someone believes it's their fault that there is hunger and poverty in the Third World and thinks, "I didn't donate enough money." The reasoning that no single person could have enough money to eradicate hunger and poverty does not count. Of course this is irrational thinking, but many people who personalise everything can get to these extremes. In domestic violence situations the victims often take the blame for the abuse. They feel it is their fault that their partner hits them. The abuser takes full advantage of this personalisation and tells them "you made me do it".

Blaming is the reverse situation. Instead of accepting responsibility for our actions, we shift it to others. We make a mistake because someone talked to us and distracted us. We hit the hammer on our thumb because our partner was standing next to us. The basic thinking behind this distortion is that someone has to take responsibility for everything. Personalisation and blaming operate on the basis that there is no such thing as a mistake or a mishap, there are only crimes and the culprits must be found and punished at all costs.

*We either accept the blame for everything or pass it
on to others. Someone has got to be guilty of the crimes.*

Combating Negative Automatic Thoughts

Let's just quickly recapture what we have learned so far. CBT is based upon the theory that emotions, behaviour and thoughts interrelate and that they are influenced by external stimuli from the past, (i.e., from our childhood), and the present. CBT suggests that psychological and emotional distress can be caused by distorted thoughts about outside events, which can lead to damaging behaviour. Now we come to the point where we can start doing something about our depressive moods. We often wrongly believe that by attempting to change outside events, such as other people's behaviour, we will feel better and our life will improve. However, it is not other people, things, or situations that hurt, hinder or control us, but our own attitudes and reactions to these outside events. Events come about as they do and people behave according to their own attitudes and the situations they are faced with. We cannot always choose external circumstances, but we can choose how we react to them.

Our thought process has an immense influence on our lives and negative thoughts are strongly associated with depression. Therefore, it is only logical that in order to manage depression it is important that we first bring about change in our thinking patterns. It is possible to take back control of our lives by slowly controlling our thought processes. It may take some time and be a bit challenging at first, but it will result in positive changes in our emotions and our behaviour. Try it now! We have nothing to lose, but our depression.

With CBT we learn to shoot down our negative automatic thoughts.

Spring Cleaning the Mind

If we compare our mind to a house we have lived in all our lives we will notice that, just like in a real house, we have accumulated a lot of old stuff over the years. Our mental house has become very cluttered and the living space is getting cramped. We need to get rid of some of the old stuff that we don't need anymore and maybe rearrange and upgrade some of the mental "furniture" to create more breathing space. If we've never done a mental clean out then those cupboards and drawers are stuffed full with ideas, beliefs, presumptions, prejudices and automatic thoughts. There is stuff we just keep on using without putting much thought into why it is still there in our mind.

CBT is firstly about examining our thoughts, beliefs, attitudes and expectations. And secondly, it is about updating outdated thinking and reactions and throwing out what is no longer of any use, or even damaging. It is time to open the windows and doors and let some fresh air and sunlight into the stuffy rooms. In a sense, with CBT we are spring cleaning our mind and thoughts. Like with every good spring-cleaning, we first need to get a broom and sweep the place out thoroughly.

We take a piece of paper and write down everything that comes into our mind about our life, our goals, achievements and us.

How do you see yourself?

What do you think your position in life is?

How high do you rate your achievements?

Write down ten words that describe you best.

What are the bad things you say about yourself?

What are the most common words or phrases you use?

What are your talents?

What are your shortcomings?

What do you think other people say about you?

What is your situation at the moment?

What do you like about it?

What don't you like about it?

What do you wish you could change?

During this process, we should just let the thoughts flow until we can't think of anything anymore. The list will give us a fairly accurate picture of our automatic thought process. Do not be surprised if mostly negative stuff comes out. When we suffer from depression, we are more likely to rate our achievements and our lives negatively. The first automatic thought we usually uncover is only the tip of the iceberg. The majority of unproductive thoughts and beliefs are hidden deep within our minds and it takes time to bring them all out into the open. If we ask ouselves what it would mean if a certain automatic thought were true, we will uncover the next one, until we have brought out the whole cluster leading to the original automatic thought, also known as a core belief (see our chapter on Core Beliefs). For example:

1) My friend has stood me up.
   Why is this upsetting to me? What does it mean?

2) It means she/he had something better to do?
   And suppose that were true, what would that mean to me?

3) I'm not important enough.
   What would that mean to me?

4) I'm worthless. (Core Belief)

It is a good idea to repeat this exercise with the different automatic thoughts and at regular intervals, once a week or at least once a month.

It is a good idea to clean out all those negative thoughts on a regular basis.

Examining Our Automatic Thoughts — Is What I Believe True?

We now have lists with the sort of thoughts and mindsets (opinions, beliefs and assumptions) that crowd our minds. They are all jumbled together and not making much sense. Therefore, it is time to start organising these thoughts and mindsets into what is still useful, what is not and what we are unsure of. We examine each one more closely and weigh it up for accuracy and usefulness by asking a series of questions, such as:

- What evidence do I base this thought/mindset on?
- Is this thought/mindset accurate?
- Is there any evidence to suggest that this thought/mindset may not be accurate?
- What are the advantages when I have these kind of thoughts/mindsets?
- What are the disadvantages?
- Is there a more realistic and positive way to look at the situation that led to this thought/mindset?
- What would be the worst thing that could happen in this situation?
- What are the chances that the worst will happen in this situation?
- What else could happen in this situation?
- What percentage of the people I know believe that this negative thought (for example, that I am dumb, ugly, incompetent, etc) or mindset is accurate.
- Are these people important to me?
- Why is it important to me that these people have a high opinion of me?

We can start to take an inventory of our automatic thoughts and the answers to the above questions. We can organise the contents into groups. We can make lists of our beliefs, convictions and opinions and map out how they relate to each other. We will probably be surprised when we find out how some of our strongest beliefs or mindsets originated and the flimsy evidence they are based on.

For example one of our mindsets may say that we are "clumsy". To find out if this is true we look at the evidence:

Question	Answer
Have we broken anything?	*We broke a cup.*
What were the circumstances	*We slipped and dropped the cup.*
How often do we handle breakable things?	*Many times every day.*
How often do we break things?	*Very rarely.*

Conclusion: We handle coffee cups and other breakable things every day and have only broken a cup once because we slipped. It was an accident. Therefore, the tag that we are clumsy is not justified.

If certain mind-sets, or thoughts, are not supported by facts or they no longer apply, then it is time to throw them out into the rubbish bin. With other thoughts, we may need to test them out before we can decide to discard them or keep them. For example, if we have the automatic thought, "I can't sing", it might be an idea to take some singing lessons before we accept the fact that we can't sing. There will also be thoughts that are useful and help us in our daily lives, such as "I am a good organiser", or "I am a reliable person". Of course these types of thoughts are those that we can keep and develop further.

We can sort the different mindsets out, some we may have to test to see if they are accurate or not, others which are negative and no longer apply we throw away.

Counters — Challenging Old Beliefs

Now that we have identified some of our automatic thoughts/mindsets and investigated if they are accurate and useful, the next step is to replace the negative automatic thoughts/mindsets with positive ones. It is common knowledge that old negative habits cannot just be eliminated without implementing new positive habits to take their place. If you take something away and leave a void, the old negative habit will quickly return. For every negative thought we want to get rid of, we need to develop a counter thought.

A counter is a thought that argues against the negative thought. It includes thinking and behaving in an opposite direction to the negative thought, in other words in the positive direction. Just like in a courtroom, we have to argue our case as to why the negative automatic thought is no longer sustainable. We have to bring out the evidence that supports our argument and convince the judge and jury, which in this case is us, just how false a certain belief is.

Counters stop the negative flow of thought dead in its tracks. It is like pulling the emergency brakes on a too fast moving train. Counters give the mind a moment to think and question those negative automatic

Just like a lawyer we have to argue our case as to why an old negative automatic thought should be replaced with a new positive thought.

thoughts that want to control us. Counters say, "wait a minute, let's just look at this more rationally." Counters ask questions:

- Am I getting the REAL picture here or a false one?
- Is this belief rational or irrational when looking at the facts?
- Does this belief serve a purpose? Do I feel better, achieve more or get along with others better because of it?
- Do I always think or believe this in similar situations?

When we use a counter we slow down the emotions before these gain too much momentum and run in a negative direction. Counters help us to be more assertive against internal or external negativity.

Counters are like automatic thoughts except they are positive in contents and processing. Good counters are:

- Short and concise. ("I am smart!")
- Believable and realistic. ("I achieve good grades", but not "I am a genius")
- Personally relevant and meaningful. (Concern "me", not others)
- Developed by us rather than someone else. ("I believe I am smart, not someone else said I was smart").
- Can be used to combat negative Automatic Thoughts. ("I am smart and capable, therefore I am NOT useless)

Learning to apply counters is very liberating and allows our true personality to come to the forefront. Just like with automatic thoughts the iceberg analogy can be applied here too; the real truths, our true assets and positive qualities are often hidden far beneath the surface with only the tip being visible. With counters we can bring them to the top, develop these positives further and build on them. The more we use counters the more they become ingrained in our thinking routine and the better we are equipped to stay in control and cope when faced with daily stresses.

Just like with distorted thoughts, there are different kinds of counters we can apply to different negative beliefs. Let's have a look at the some of the counters we can use in everyday situations.

Direct Counters - It is Not True!

A direct counter is the simplest form of counter. It acts directly against a negative automatic thought. It doesn't need to list reasons or evidence, because it flatly and firmly denies the accuracy of the negative statement.

For example:

Automatic Thought	Direct Counter
"I am stupid"	"I am NOT stupid" or "I AM intelligent"
"I am a bad person"	"I am a GOOD person"
"I am worthless"	"I am NOT worthless"

When we use this counter we know that the negative belief or mindset is false. We just have to strengthen this knowledge. With the direct counter we smash the negative statement/mindset or automatic thought with one precise and powerful hit. These type of counters are excellent to use as a first line of defence. We stand up to our negative automatic thoughts and refuse to give them any nourishment to multiply and thereby create a whole cluster of negative thoughts. By repeating the direct counter we can reinforce it in our minds and stop the flow of negative thoughts before they can send us further into depression.

With a direct counter we state a certain fact .

Ordinary Counters – Looking at the Evidence

With ordinary counters we give a reason as to why we are arguing against a certain statement and offer some factual evidence to counter the false automatic thought. We can find the evidence that will counter the negative automatic thought by:

- using our senses (what we see, hear, can feel, taste, smell)
- asking an authority (our partner, our doctor or therapist)
- finding out what most people think (our friends, family)
- using reason and logic (common sense)
- using our own experiences (have we experienced this or something similar before?)

For example:

"I am not stupid, *BECAUSE* I have a demanding job that takes a lot of know-how to perform" or "I have achieved good grades in my studies".

"I am not useless, *BECAUSE* I contribute to my family's wellbeing by taking care of them and thereby I contribute to society at large".

"I am not worthless *BECAUSE* I am a caring human being and I have a loving partner, family and friends who all think highly of me and support me".

We closely examine the evidence supporting an automatic thought.

Alternative Explanations - What Else is There?

We all jump to conclusions too quickly and accept the first possible explanation that pops into our minds as a given fact. If we are having trouble with our moods, then the first reason will most likely be negative and personalised. For example: "our friend didn't call, so he or she must be mad at me". With alternative explanations we try to find other reasons as to why something happened, or didn't happen.

For example:

She didn't call
- because she may have had to work late.
- because she may have had a family emergency.
- because she was busy and forgot.

My boss is cranky
- because he may have personal problems.
- because he broke down with the car.
- because he is not feeling well.

These are all plausible conclusions that can be drawn from the same information and they have nothing to do with us. Therefore there is a strong possibility that our first conclusion "she didn't call because she is mad at me" or "my boss is cranky because I've done something wrong" could be false.

We look for other reasons why something happened.

80

Decatostrophising - What are the Facts?

Although we tend to think the worst when depressed, in the majority of cases, the worst never happens. The process of decatastrophising involves re-evaluating the situation and analysing the contents of the thoughts, then rating them for probability. The catastrophic thought and the probability are then compared to previous 'catastrophic' predictions and the accuracy of their fulfillment. For example, we are stuck in traffic and are afraid of running late for an important business meeting. If we are catastrophising, our thought process may be as follows: "I'm going to miss my appointment, I won't get the business deal and then I will lose my job and I won't be able to make a living and I'll end up on the street". Before we know it anxiety starts to build up, we get agitated and may even start to panic. The perfect breeding ground for depression.

By decatastrophising the thought process, we are encouraged to let our thoughts flow in the other direction: "If I am a couple of minutes late, they will understand. This won't hinder me making the business deal. I've run late before because of traffic or other reasons and everyone understood. If other people run late for an appointment with me I always wait and they usually have a very plausible explanation. The chances of me losing my job and ending up on the street are very slim". We have looked at the catastrophic thought process from a realistic perspective and found that it is highly unlikely that anything bad is going to happen.

We list all the known facts of a given situation.

81

Coping Statements — I Can Handle This!

Another type of counter is the coping statement. Here we actually assume the worst, then talk ourselves through the situation. We look at other avenues and other possibilities. Let us stay with the example of losing our job. What are our options?

- We could look for a new job, maybe a better paid one.

- Maybe we have special skills that are rare in our field of work and we could start our own business.

- We could change career and do something else that gives us pleasure.

- We could go back to school and acquire new qualifications.

By looking at the unknown and establishing a coping strategy, the worst-case scenario doesn't look that daunting anymore. Every top athlete, or successful business person, will confirm that they regularly look at what could go wrong and then choose the best alternative route. If the worst does occur, they remain calm and focused because they know what to do. The same applies to everyday life. Knowing that we could cope takes away the fear and the panic.

*We look at the worst that could happen
and decide what we could do if it were reality.*

Philosophical Counters — What is Done is Done!

Here we focus on what serves a purpose and what doesn't. Once the milk is spilt, there's no use crying about it. What are we going to achieve if we put ourselves down because we spilt a glass of milk? Nothing! We can't undo the mishap and we can't get the milk back into the glass because it is spilt all over the floor. Lamenting and blaming ourselves for something that has already happened has no advantage and serves no purpose. Being philosophical about it is the best approach. Accept it and move on.

It is better to invest our energies in finding a solution to a problem and learning from an event, so that it doesn't happen again in the future. In other words, we should clean up the mess and get another glass of milk, being more careful with it the next time. Sometimes our reactions to a negative event are far worse than the event itself warrants. For example, yelling at our partner because he or she put a dent in the car will not make the situation any better. On the contrary, they will feel worse than they already do and we are now adding relationship problems to the mix. If we accept that mistakes happen and even the smartest people can sometimes do dumb things, then we are ready to accept occasional mishaps as part of life and be more equipped to deal with them in a positive manner.

Sometimes dumb things happen. It is no big deal.
Accept it and move on.

Label-Shifting - What Can I Learn from This?

Shifting the labels we use to describe situations or events, from being negative, then to neutral, then to positive, will help counter some of our negative automatic thoughts. It's like shifting the gears in a car, you don't go from low to high in one move, you always shift past neutral. For example, a person might have the label of being bossy. When you shift labels you can argue that the person is only standing up for their rights (neutral), therefore they are not bossy but assertive (positive). Or imagine we've done something wrong. Now instead of labeling ourselves as an idiot, we acknowledge that we are human and that humans make mistakes (neutral). The positive spin on this would be that mistakes are there to teach us a better way (positive).

Sometimes mistakes can lead to something good. History is full of examples where discoveries have been made by mistake. Penicillin was discovered because culture plates were left unwashed. If it hadn't been for this apparent carelessness it might have taken many decades longer until the antibiotic would have been discovered. Over the decades Penicillin has saved millions of lives. So let us not be so quick to label ourselves as idiots when we make a mistake. You never know - that mistake might lead to something good.

We learn most from our mistakes therefore something negative can become a good experience.

Humorous Counters - See the Funny Side of Things

Nothing can take the sting out of negativity as fast as a touch of humour. The most content people are the ones who can laugh at their own mistakes and themselves. The ability to not take negative events, or one's own shortcomings, too seriously is a great way to counter those dysfunctional thought patterns. With a bit of fun we bring events back into a more realistic perspective and our mood improves immediately.

Imagine we have tripped over something and fallen flat on our face. Now we can curse and blame somebody for leaving out the blasted thing that was in our way, or we can put our annoyance aside for a minute and step back and look at the situation from the outside. It may not be dignified lying on the ground with our face in the mud, but it sure looks funny. In a few days, we will be retelling the story to our friends and having a good laugh.

Humorous quotations are a great way to ward off negative thoughts:

Thought: "I am useless because I can't solve problems."
Quotation: *"Intellectuals solve problems; geniuses prevent them."*
                                            (Albert Einstein)

Thought: "I haven't finished school that's why I am dumb."
Quotation: *"I have never let my schooling interfere with my education."*
                                            (Mark Twain)

Some things are just too funny to be taken seriously.
A hearty laugh lifts the mood in an instant.

Existential Counters — Sometimes Things Just Turn Out for the Best

Many dysfunctional thoughts are based on old beliefs, rules or regulations that were once valid and have since become generalisations. Very few of these negative automatic thoughts are based on solid facts. The counters also don't have to be based on facts. For example, we have the negative thought that we are worthless. What do we base that belief on? What is the value of a human life? In today's society, a human being is worthwhile simply by just existing. So everything we do to make a difference, like doing our job well, adds to our worth. Or the question "why me?" can be countered with the thought "Why not me?" The majority of people will be confronted with depression at some stage in their lives. Is it therefore surprising that we are grappling with it at present? It was just our turn. Maybe it can teach us something.

A happy life is not just about experiencing highs, but also riding the lows and enjoying the journey. It is about seeing what is on the other side of the fence and then trying to deal with it in a beneficial way. It is about learning something from every challenge, stretching ourselves just that bit further. If something negative is not within our control to change, then we sometimes need to trust in the future and hope that things will sort themselves out. And many times life has magical powers.

Life can make things happen as if it were pulling a rabbit out of a hat.

Problem Solving — What Can I Do About It?

After we have discovered how to turn negative thoughts into positive ones with the help of counters we can look at another contributor to our depression; our problems. Throughout our lives we are regularly confronted with problems, but when we are depressed problems seem to be appearing everywhere. This is because when we are depressed we are less able to deal with the demands and stresses of everyday life. Our coping mechanism is not functioning properly and minor upsets become major issues. Therefore it is important that we learn to deal with problems in a more objective and productive way.

Let's take a closer look at how we can deal with problems. Some problems are easy to solve, some are seemingly minor at first glance, but take a while to tackle. Then there are problems that are beyond our capacity to resolve, like poverty, the threat of terrorism or natural disasters. No matter how perfect our life is, there will always be times when problems pop up. As strange as it may sound, problems are actually good for us. A life without any problems is a dull existence. History proves that progress has always been brought about by the desire, or need, to solve problems. A problem is an opportunity to change something and hopefully make it better. If we look at a problem more as a challenge our entire attitude towards it changes and we may suddenly see possibilities where there were only obstacles before.

It sometimes takes a while to figure out how to fit a square peg into a round hole.

1. Do I Have a Problem?

Before we start solving a problem, it would be a good idea to firstly determine if the situation or circumstance we are in is actually a problem or not. If it isn't a problem, don't make into one. Life is demanding enough without us putting more obstacles in our own way. If it is out of your control then don't worry about it. It will solve itself when the time is right. To establish if we have a problem we need to ask ourselves the following questions:

a) Frequency – How Often Does It Happen?

Problems have a tendency to keep on popping up until we find a solution. For example, if every time we bend down to pick something up our back goes out of joint we have a problem. However, if we drop a hammer on our toe then we may have a very painful incident, but we most likely won't have a problem because hopefully we won't be dropping the hammer on our toe again. If something only happens once, we don't have to find a solution because the situation will not occur again. But if something keeps on happening again and again, like our back becoming sore when we bend down, we need to solve the problem, perhaps by seeing a doctor and getting our back fixed.

If our back hurts everytime we bend down we have a problem.

b) Duration — When It Happens How Long Does It Last?

Problems usually last long enough to bother us. If something only lasts a short time, like when we bump our head and it hurts for a couple of minutes, it is best to just endure it and then it is over, therefore it isn't a problem. However, if our back is out of joint and we can't straighten up for hours or even days afterwards, we have a problem and need to do something about it. Problems must last long enough to cause trouble in our life in a major, or minor, way. Ask yourself a few basic questions to determine the problem's duration:

How long has this problem been bothering me?

Why has this problem been bothering me?

What are the disadvantages if I don't solve this problem now?

What are the advantages if I do solve this problem now?

If I do nothing, will this problem go away by itself?

How often has this problem occured in the past?

Am I willing to face this problem again in the future?

If we can't move without feeling pain for hours, we have a problem.

c) Severity — When It Happens How Bad is It?

The severity of a problem can range from a minor upset to extreme disaster and can seriously disrupt our everyday life and future wellbeing. Some problems are more annoying than distressing and we may be able to live with it if necessary, like when the neighbour's dog barks all night. But if a something really causes us distress, physically, socially or financially, then we can assume we have a problem. Coming back to our example of a bad back, maybe the pain in our back is so bad that we feel dizzy and sick. If it is just a small twitch we won't be in a hurry to see a doctor. But if the pain is excruciating and we can't sit, stand or lie down without pain we will need to find a solution for our problem soon.

When the problem occurs what are the consequences for me?

Can I live with the consequences/effects of the problem?

How seriously does this problem disrupt my life?

Will I be happier/my life run smoother if I solve this problem?

Is the improvement in life quality worth the effort of solving the problem?

*If the problem is really painful, literally or metaphorically,
we need to do something about it.*

d) Cost — When It Happens What Does It Cost Us?

This is the impact the problem has on our life emotionally, psychologically, financially and maybe even in relationship terms. Not being able to get out of bed and walk straight, means we won't be able to meet our obligations; and we won't be much fun to be around either, because we will be cranky and irritable, which may in turn lead to arguments. Therefore, we are paying a price emotionally and in our relationship. We may also be paying a financial price if we don't solve the problem, for example with a bad back we can't work and money isn't coming in. Or the problem can cost us psychologically, because we may feel dependent on others and useless when we are immobile, or because we can't do certain things and we believe we are letting others down. The effects of a problem can ripple further and further out, even into other people's lives, until we start to solve it.

We must also evaluate what it will cost us to solve the problem and relate this to the benefit. If the doctor's quote for treatment is exorbitant and there is a good chance our back will heal with rest, then it might be better not to solve the problem. Or the neighbour's dog is only barking because it is sick or frightened to be alone. If the dog's barking is a one-off thing we must ask ourselves if it is worth it to upset the good neighbourly relations.

We need to assess how much it will cost us
if we do or if we don't solve the problem.

2. Look at the Problem from a Different Angle

Once we have established that we have a problem we can look at it more closely. When we are depressed, problems often seem insurmountable and overwhelming. This is because if we stand too close to an obstacle it becomes gigantic. We can also get lost in the minute details, while the problem looms over us and seems to grow every time we glance at it. We feel as if the problem is devouring us and taking over our life. What do we do? When facing a problem it is often best to step back and examine it from a distance, or from a different angle.

It is sometimes all a matter of perspective. Looking down on a problem means that we can become aware of the surroundings and the particular circumstances which have led to the problem. From this viewpoint, the problem often appears less frightening and solvable. What has contributed to the problem? Where does change need to be made so that the problem becomes solvable? If we have financial problems we might need to ask ourselves if we are spending a lot of money for things we don't really need. Maybe we are not keeping track of our spending on credit cards or how much we are withdrawing from the bank. If we look at the problem from the other angle we might discover that we are not earning enough to meet our needs. We need to take in the bigger picture.

A) If we stand too close to a problem it often seems overwhelming.
B) Looking at a problem from a different perspective sometimes makes it smaller.

3. Identify the Problem — What is It Exactly I am Not Happy with?

We have become aware of the circumstances that led to the problem, let's start to identify the finer details. It is easier to solve a specific problem than a vague one. Therefore, it is important to clarify the problem before looking for a solution. We can identify key elements of the problem by asking ourselves questions about the problem, and clearly detailing what we are unhappy with and what we actually want. Problems are often accompanied with a varying amount of useless information. We need to sift through this and throw out the garbage by asking a few questions:

Why is this a problem?

What are the facts of the problem?

What do I want to achieve? (Be realistic about your expectations.)

Can I break this problem up into smaller, managable parts?

How urgent is the problem? Can it wait or do I need to solve it now?

If our problem is that our spouse is not attentive enough, we need to specify exactly what we expect from him or her. Or if our problem is financial, we need to write down exactly what we need more money for, how we spend our money, and how much more money we need to solve the problem. Put a figure on the problem or give it a name.

If we know exactly what the problem is and throw out the useless information, it will be easier to solve it.

4. Choose a Strategy — How Can I Solve It?

If we don't make a plan or choose a strategy to solve a problem, then we may be heading off in the wrong direction and waste time and energy. When choosing a strategy to solve a problem, experience is a good guide. Have we solved similar problems in the past? If yes, we can look at the strategies we had chosen and their outcome. Maybe we can take the same strategies and modify them slightly to solve the current problem. Or we may need to work out a new plan. Strategies don't have to be perfect. Sometimes we have to choose a strategy, which solves the problem in a roundabout way. If the problem is too big, we might need to break it up into different parts and solve it one step at a time.

The purpose of a strategy is to give us a starting point and general direction. It is not carved in stone and does not have to be followed at any cost. Most of the time, we will be fine-tuning our solution as we go along. The space shuttle didn't fly to the moon in a straight line: it had to adjust its direction countless times. Therefore, it is not important and in fact, highly unlikely, that a strategy can guarantee the desired result. But if it seems as though it might work, it is worth trying. If it doesn't work, then it may just lead us to a strategy that will work.

*Making a plan as to how to solve the problem
gives us a starting point and a guideline.*

5. Put Your Plan into Action

Implementing our chosen strategy is the best way to find out what works and what doesn't. It is important that we are not afraid of making mistakes. Mistakes are not failures, but opportunities to make something different or better. Mistakes entice us to challenge, change and correct situations. Just as problems are our friends, mistakes are our mentors. They keep our mind active and constantly add new experiences. We learn more from mistakes than we do from our successes. The only failure is to not do anything. Sometimes the wrong plan is just a stepping stone to the right plan. Solving problems promotes independent thinking, it teaches us perserverance and helps us to develop our reasoning and evaluation skills. We learn intellectual courage, determination and flexibility.

It is important to recognise that not all problems are solvable. Not being able to find a solution for a problem has no reflection upon our character or our abilities. Sometimes the time isn't right for a problem or it has to sit and simmer until it lends itself to a solution. Some problems you can put in a box and let life or fate solve it for you. Then there are also situations and circumstances, such as a natural disaster or a handicap, which cannot be resolved but only accepted.

Sometimes the plan needs to be slightly
adjusted to solve the problem.

6. Look Back and Reflect

When we have solved the problem, it is time to look back on it and evaluate it and its solution. We can reflect on how bad the problem really was in hindsight and what it took to solve it. We might find that once we have clearly identified the problem, its solution was maybe obvious, or at least not as hopeless as we had anticipated.

It is advisable that we log the problem and the solution into our memory for future reference and as a reminder that we ACTUALLY CAN solve problems. It is even a good idea to keep a written record of the problem and its successful solution. Then we can easily refer back to it if a similar problem occurs in the future. The successful handling of a problem is another notch on our experience belt and having been able to eliminate one problem not only makes our life easier it also gives us the confidence to face the future with more enthusiasm.

Remember when solving problems that we can only try to make the best decision based on information that is available at the time when the decision is made. If further information becomes available later we may be able to alter our plan or decision accordingly. However, it is a mistake to judge a decision on its outcome. Foresight and hindsight are two different things.

When we've solved the problem we can and should be proud of our achievement.

Core Beliefs and the Functioning of the Mind

As mentioned in our chapter on 'Automatic Thoughts', what we learn and experience in our early life does have an effect on how we see the world in later life. All of the information, which has generated some feelings within us, gets catalogued and filed away. In a sense, an internal memory map is created and throughout our lifetime we use this map to understand the world and our role in it.

Whether our future and our expectation of it will be positive depends largely on our emotional interpretation of past and future events, in other words, on our memories about the past and/or our expectations about the future. For example, a baby cries. It gets picked up, it is soothed, cuddled and cooed over and told it is beautiful. Now this baby is going to experience good feelings. Therefore, making one's presence felt, (i.e. by crying), will be associated with being soothed and cuddled and the baby will lay down a good memory. And if this happens again and again, the good feelings will be reinforced. So this baby will have the expectation that it will be picked up and soothed when it cries. Thereby this child learns that it is okay to express his or her needs. The child will register this as a fact and it establishes what the professional calls a "schema", or core belief in its mind that says, "I am important and valuable".

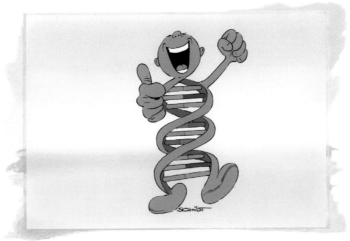

Although the Optimistic Gene hasn't been discovered some people are more optimistic than others.

Core Beliefs Give Structure to our Thinking

Core beliefs act like mental structures in our thinking patterns. They uphold our beliefs, personal values, social values and perceptions of our environment and us. These structures channel the information we receive from our environment, evaluate it and give it a meaning. Core beliefs are created by our memories of things we were taught, or have experienced. If we have felt very strong emotions at the time the core belief was created, then the more powerful this core belief will become. Core beliefs influence our behaviour and reactions on a subconscious level. Most of the time we have no idea where certain beliefs came from. The child who has established the "I am important and valuable" core belief in infancy will as an adult hardly remember how or when this belief was formed.

Core beliefs, positive and negative, are often handed down from one generation to the next. In old Europe feuds sometimes lasted centuries. The core belief "they are my enemy" was firmly engraved in the feuding participants' minds and determined how they reacted to one another. Core beliefs can also lay dormant for years and then arise with surprising force when compatible information is received. Once a core belief is established, any information that supports it will also reinforce it. If the core beliefs are positive they give us confidence and empower us, if they are negative they can cripple our progress and happiness.

Core Beliefs build the structure which supports our ideas, beliefs and opinions.

98

Are Core Beliefs the Same as Automatic Thoughts?

At first glance it may seem that core beliefs and automatic thoughts are the same thing. Although negative core beliefs and our own negative automatic thoughts seem to feed off each other and can both conjure up strong emotions, they are essentially different. Automatic thoughts are the bits of information that are fed into our mind, while core beliefs represent the track that this information follows to lead us to have predetermined reactions. For example, if a friend doesn't say hello to us on the street, the automatic thought may be, "she or he is mad at me" but it may follow along the track to lead to the "Nobody likes me" core belief and we will feel disheartened and depressed.

A person who experienced positive reinforcement and encouragement in their early life will establish positive core beliefs and will more likely become an optimist. In other words, this person will be able to tackle life's problems in a more confident manner. If anyone in the future tells him or her that they are stupid and useless, they will seriously question the validity of the statement because it goes against their established perception that says, "I am valuable and important". If a person simply does not have any core beliefs marked "stupid and useless", then this type of information will either not go through at all, or it will arrive as a very weak signal in their mind.

Core beliefs determine how we see ourselves.

99

Repeating Negative Core Beliefs Amplifies their Effect

Of course this process works the other way around too. If a person is mainly criticised, discouraged, or told they can't do something, even labeled as dumb and useless, the associated feelings are more likely going to be negative. Consequently, negative core beliefs are created. The possibilities of this person becoming discouraged and a pessimist are greatly increased. In their mind, they will accept as an actual fact, that they are dumb and useless. Likewise, if someone in the future tells them that they are smart and capable, they will also seriously question the validity of this statement because they have no core beliefs marked "smart and capable". This positive information will either be completely ignored or minimised.

If incoming information finds a corresponding core belief in the mind, then the message will be further amplified and the more frequently the same message gets transmitted, the more it gets amplified. For example, if the incoming information is "you are useless" and a "you are useless" core belief already exists, then the "you are useless" message will echo in your mind several decibels louder than it was meant to. Every time an incoming message supports an existing core belief, the groove digs just a bit deeper. Well-established core beliefs not only become harder to dislodge, but their influence on our life is continually increased.

*If the same negative message gets repeated
over and over again we hear it louder everytime.*

Examine Your Negative Core Beliefs

It has been established that upbringing does have a profound effect on whether or not we are going to become an optimist, or a pessimist, in later life. However, if we have experienced a less than positive childhood we are not doomed forever and ever to experience life from a negative position. The good news is that core beliefs are learned processes; therefore we can relearn new core beliefs and start to change those damaging negative ones.

The basic principles used to help us change negative perceptions about our self are quite simple. We need to examine the validity of those old core beliefs. We can start to question our toxic beliefs with the help of counters (see chapter on "Counters"). If we believe we are useless, then we must ask ourselves why we think this? What evidence do we have to suggest that we are useless? Where did this core belief come from? Maybe someone who wasn't competent to judge or didn't like us was the one who told us we were useless. We can also list all the things in our private and professional life that we wouldn't be able to do if we really were useless. By asking some simple questions and finding out where this core belief came from, we can evaluate if it is really true, or if we can replace it with a more positive core belief like, "I am quite good at doing things".

If we disect negative core beliefs and look at what they are based on we can judge if they serve a purpose.

101

Change or Modify Your Negative Core Beliefs to Positive Core Beliefs

Core beliefs have a tendency to be stubborn and will resist any change initially. It is therefore necessary to keep trying to change negative core beliefs to positive ones. We can actually train ourselves to become optimists. It just takes a bit of time, some courage and a determination to change.

Some core beliefs may have served a purpose once, but the circumstances for which they were created no longer exist. For example, if we grew up in an abusive family, we may have learnt the core belief "to hide when arguments start brewing". This tactic served us well as a child because we didn't get beaten while we were hiding. In the meantime we have grown up, we no longer live in the same environment and the "go and hide" core belief should actually be discarded. But it may still influence our behaviour subconsciously. If we run at the first sign of an argument, we won't be able to stand up for our rights, we won't learn to be assertive and some people might bully us or take advantage of us. Therefore, the core belief that was set up to protect us has actually become a hindrance. It is time to maybe change the core belief from "go and hide" to "stay and talk things through".

*If a core belief no longer serves a positive
purpose we can either replace it or modify it.*

Using Mantras to Create Positive Core Beliefs

Many, if not all, negative core beliefs are rarely based on facts, but are simply based on what we perceive to be the facts. In the same way, our objections to existing negative core beliefs don't always need to be based on facts either. Sometimes putting the cart before the horse is the only way to get rid of persistent negative core beliefs. The trick is to continually tell ourselves that we are capable of doing something even though we may still feel insecure. Using the mantra "I can do this", over and over again, will start to inject positive vibes into our mind. With time we will not only start to believe we can do something, but we will actually be able to do it. It doesn't matter if the task is not perfect, what is important is that we have taken positive action that will bring a positive result.

When we are questioning our negative core beliefs we will notice that certain counters can be applied to various situations and we can use them again and again. It is a good idea to turn these counters into mantras, or regularly repeated mental statements. For example, a philosophical counter like "things are never as bad as they first look", is an excellent mantra, or mental statement to use over and over again, when facing difficult situations. Or telling yourself every day how important you are to those you love will help you think more of yourself.

We can establish positive core beliefs by repeating them again and again like a mantra.

Changing the Negative Memories of the Past

One of the major causes of depression is trauma or negative life events. Maybe we were in a car accident, robbery or had to survive in a war zone or an abusive family. Because these events are so deeply engraved in our memories, we experience emotional pain every time we think about them and subsequently become more depressed. But what if we could change the memory of the past? You might say that "the past is past" or, "how can one change the memory of something that has already happened?"

Our memories retain the emotions we experienced at the time(s) of the negative life events. In crime investigations, why is it that the victims or witnesses often have difficulties remembering facts such as height or hair colour of the perpetrator, or the make of a car? Because they were too busy coping with the emotions flooding their system. Even though the facts can become decisively blurry as time passes, we can often remember exactly how terrified we were, or how much pain we felt. This is because our memories are mainly comprised of the emotions we experienced at the time the memory was created.

Human beings have a tendency to focus predominantly on the negative things of unpleasant memories. We remember the terror, the humiliation and the pain experienced during the event. What we seldom see are the positive aspects of something horrible. Everything we have experienced makes up part of who we are and nothing shapes us more than adversity. Pain and misfortune test us to the limit and quite often our strengths and resilience come to the forefront because of it. It is not uncommon for the negative happenings to change the direction we take in life and often for the better.

Changing the memory of the past is much like treating a phobia; you desensitise yourself. We cannot undo what has happened, but revisiting the past event in our mind will help us cope with the flood of emotions rather than wishing them away. It's like being afraid of spiders; you first start getting used to looking at the spider from a safe distance. Then next time you come a bit closer and count the spider's legs and look at the shape of its body. You desensitise yourself to the spider more and more until your fear has disappeared, or has at least reduced so much that you don't panic when you see a spider. You even learn that spiders eat insects and play an important role in keeping nature balanced. So spiders are actually good things in the right environment. Does this mean you are going to love spiders in the future? Probably not, but it means that spiders won't send you into an extreme state of anxiety anymore.

We can also learn to emotionally cope with traumatic events by applying the same principle. When we feel safe, maybe with a trusted friend close at hand, we can let our mind recall different aspects of the trauma. If we can look at it bit by bit it is less traumatic. Let your body feel each of those emotions, one at a time from the beginning to the end. If it gets too much stop, take a break and maybe start again later or on another day. Do not fight the emotions. Give yourself permission to feel them, let them flow out of you. Yes, you feel rotten now, but it will go away with time. By doing this you are desensitising your mind and yourself to the trauma. If you do this several times until the trauma no longer causes you the deep emotional pain and you can accept it as part of your life experience, you will discover that you have become stronger because of it. Take a sheet of paper and write down the positive things you have experienced, or what you have learned about yourself because of a misfortune. Maybe you have learnt that you are quite tough, that you have stamina and a strong willpower. Or your capacity for empathy has greatly increased. Because you have survived something distressing, you may have lost some of your fear of life and gained the confidence that you can handle things better.

*Like you can learn to not be terrified of spiders, you can also
learn to reduce the emotional pain of a trauma.*

Although his riding accident left him a quadriplegic, Christopher Reeve became an untiring advocate for spinal injury research and earned the admiration and respect of millions of people all over the world. Had he not suffered this terrible accident, would he have taken on this cause? Maybe not. Through his determination and vigour, Christopher Reeve became a shining example of a man who turned misfortune into something positive. He chose to embrace his affliction and make the best out of it. He will be a role model for many people who have faced adversity for generations to come. Without this tragedy he may have just remained the actor who played Superman.

We too can change the memory of the past by shining the spotlight on the positive things and less on the negative. An assault victim might recall the strength of mind that he or she had to have to be able to survive the attack and they can use this to their advantage in the future. Someone who grew up in an abusive family might have developed a deep compassion and empathy for people or animals in need. A victim of domestic violence might be able to see the signs of abuse in a neighbour or friend and offer help and a person who has lived with depression may recognise the symptoms in others and might just be able to save a life. Every experience changes us in some way. It is up to us how we accept the changes and make the best of them by focusing on the positive. You won't be the **SAME** person you were before the traumatic event or have the **SAME** circumstances back. But you can have something **SIMILAR**. Work on your strengths and develop these further.

Sometimes something good grows out of something bad.

BUILDING UP SELF ESTEEM

Depression and low self-esteem usually go hand in hand. Depressed people find it hard to stay convinced of their own positive attributes. They tend to belittle their abilities and downgrade their achievements. Self-esteem is important for our healthy functioning. Without a certain level of self-esteem we find it difficult to make the decisions and take the risks necessary in order to lead productive lives.

A low self-esteem hinders us in almost every aspect of our lives. It will sabotage personal and professional relationships, stall our careers and cloud our judgments. In some people low self-esteem manifests itself as an excessive fear of failure and they become over-competitive. Or they feel they are 'not good enough' no matter what they do and they become helpless and want someone else to take charge of their affairs and rescue them.

On the other hand, high self-esteem will strengthen our self-confidence and sharpen our problem-solving abilities. It will motivate us and give us the courage to achieve our ambitions and thus fulfill our potential. However, high self-esteem should not be confused with boasting and appearing over-confident. On the contrary, such people are more inclined to have self-esteem problems. People with a healthy level of self-esteem are happier and possess an inner tranquility. They have stronger personal relationships, are motivated and have the right attitude to succeed in life. Positive self-esteem is a self fulfilling prophecy: the more we like ourselves, the more we will act in likeable ways and the more we will be liked; the more we believe in ourselves, the more likely it is that we will achieve our goals. In other words, if we can lift our self-esteem we can weaken the grip depression has on us and experience more success in our endeavours.

What is Self-Esteem?

So the logical conclusion is that self-esteem is a good tool in the fight against depression. It is true that when we feel good about ourselves depression finds it very hard to raise its ugly head. So what is self-esteem exactly? Some may say that self-esteem is self-confidence. Although confidence is a big part of self-esteem, it is not the only part. Self–confidence is usually based on how well we have done, or how well we haven't done, in previous situations. It is based on experience. If we have accomplished a task well in the past then we will have the self-confidence that we will master the same, or a similar task, well in the future too. The outcome of past events determines how we feel about the future and ourselves.

Self-esteem, on the other hand, goes deeper. It is also about how we value ourselves as a person. And this has absolutely nothing to do with money or material possessions, although being financially secure does lift our self-confidence. We can have a high self-esteem without being rich in monetary terms. Self-esteem is also how we value the job we do and our achievements. Do we feel we are making a difference, even if it is in a small way? Self-esteem is about our attributes and skills and our acceptance of them and of our strengths and weaknesses. It is about our role in the community and how we relate to others, as well as our ability to be independent and responsible for our actions. Self-esteem is about how comfortable we feel in our skin and our environment. Positive self-esteem results in a positive self-image.

Self-esteem is how high we value our attributes, skills and characteristics.

Playing the Win-Win Game

Young children possess an enviable self-esteem. They don't question it or doubt it. Children accept themselves and others just for being people and they don't beat up on themselves when they can't do something or make mistakes. They simply try again until they get it right. Children seem to instinctively know that making mistakes is just part of the learning process. They feel proud if they partially succeed. Nearly getting there is just as good as getting there. Unfortunately, somewhere between childhood and adulthood this pure self-esteem gets eroded. The tendency to base personal value only on the result of individual situations, instead of looking at our overall performance can deflate our self-esteem. Also, we often set unrealistically high standards for ourselves and don't allow any leeway for errors, which only feeds our depression.

So how can we get the self-esteem of our childhood back and learn to value ourselves as human beings with some imperfections? We play the Win-Win game. Now this may seem a daunting task at first, but it is easier than we think. Playing the Win-Win game is played the same way as we used to play the Lose-Lose game, except from the opposite end of the spectrum. Instead of putting ourselves down, we are going to start building ourselves, and others, up and thereby improving the quality of our life.

In the Win-Win game everybody benefits.

109

Ten Steps to Positive Self-Esteem

1. Compare Yourself with Others Fairly

If we have to compare ourselves with others we should at least do it on a level playing field. When we have low self-esteem and are depressed we generally compare ourselves with people in better circumstances, which means that we compare and evaluate ourselves in a negative way. This is the Lose-Lose game and the rules are set against us from the start. We will always find people who are better off than us, richer, more successful and more attractive. Depressed people tend to make upward comparisons for good qualities, "she is so much better looking than me", and downward comparisons for negative qualities, "he doesn't have nearly as many problems as I have".

However, if we want to gain an objective view of our position in life we need to look at the other side as well. If we want to draw comparisons between ourselves and others, then why not compare ourselves with someone who is less fortunate than us. There are many people in much worse circumstances than us, with more problems and less abilities to cope. We don't need to look far to realise that we are still in quite a fortunate position, despite the hurdles we are facing. For us to build positive self-esteem it is important to learn to accept what we have and to be grateful for it.

There will always be some who have more than us.

2. Stop Putting Yourself Down!

How can we fight depression and develop high self-esteem when we regularly criticise ourselves? Repeating negative comments about our skills, abilities and ourselves generally, is like constantly hitting ourselves on the head with a hammer. We wouldn't do it to our worst enemy, why do we do it to ourselves? It may sometimes only be in jest when we call ourselves "stupid" and "useless", but our subconscious registers every time we make a negative remark about ourselves and soon it will be feeding this negative information back to us in the form of automatic thoughts. Before we know it we will believe these negative comments.

Putting ourselves down not only leads further into depression, but other people will also pick up on the negativity and take it on board. If we don't want others to have a negative view of us, we have to start seeing ourselves in a better light. Use those "buts" and turn them into positives. For example, "We may be having a hard time now, BUT it will get better soon". We can do the same to those debilitating "what if" remarks. We can turn them around and give them a positive edge. "What if we can do that job and achieve that goal." Learning to recognise those putting-down comments and changing the process so that it works in our favour will support a positive self-image. Now, if we can accept our mistakes as part of the developing process, which will ultimately lead us to more innovative solutions, then we are off to a brighter future.

Why Do we keep beating up on ourselves? We only make our depression worse.

3. Make it a Habit to Use Positive Affirmations

In the Lose-Lose game, we have programmed our mind to repeat negative phrases about ourselves, and look how that worked. We became depressed. In the Win-Win game, we start getting into the habit of thinking and saying positive things about us to others and ourselves. We could write our positive affirmations on bits of paper and stick them to the dashboard of our car, on our computer screen or on the bathroom mirror. If we don't want other people to know what we're doing, we can abbreviate these good affirmations or make associations. For example, a smiley face on our coffee mug may remind us that we are happy and fun to be around.

While we are building up our self-esteem we are allowed to shamelessly exaggerate our good qualities in the beginning and we don't necessarily need any definite proof that these good things are really true. For starters we will just assume that they are true. After all, most of the negative stuff we used to tell ourselves wasn't true either. Positive affirmations will encourage us to try to live up to our expectations, for example:

"Things are going really well for me today."

"I am happier today than I was yesterday and tomorrow I will be even happier still."

Repeating our good points and acting on them can build up self-esteem and weaken our depression.

4. Accept Compliments Graciously

It is amazing how many of us are reluctant to accept a compliment. When someone compliments us we blush, become self-conscious and embarrassed. If we have trouble with depression we are even more inclined to reject a compliment. It is quite possible that we may even become hostile and angry. So how can someone else see something good in us when we only see the bad things? The answer lies in the clarity of vision. They have a clear view of our attributes and qualities, whereas we see ourselves only through the murkiness of our depression.

Anyway, why should we be embarrassed when someone recognises a good quality in us? By ignoring or dismissing a compliment we not only deny ourselves a precious gift, but we also deny the giver the gift of giving. Refusing to accept a compliment conveys to other people the message that we don't deserve, or are not worthy, of praise. Subsequently, other people will become more hesitant to praise us and acknowledge our achievements and abilities in the future. Remember, we teach others how to treat us; if we treat ourselves badly what example are we giving them? In our fast paced society, compliments are rare and should be treated as something very special. Both the giver and the receiver of the compliment can enjoy the positive sentiments and build up their self-esteem.

Every compliment we receive is a precious gift
for the receiver as well as the giver.

5. Mix with Positive and Supportive People

Nothing can sap our positive energies faster than negative people and when we are struggling with depression they can just about flatten us. Whoever we associate with will influence our thoughts, our actions and our behaviour. Negative people who put our achievements and our ideas down will lower our self-esteem. No matter what we say and how determined we are to stay positive our negative "friends" will always have a "but" at the end of it and deflate any good intentions we might have had. It is nearly impossible to stay positive if our environment is negative.

Life is so much easier around positive and supportive people. The impossible seems to become possible. They can help to build us up and to stay focused on our goal, even when we are plagued with self-doubt. In the company of people with a good outlook on life, mountains are turned into molehills and positive, supportive friends and family are the soft place to land when the going gets tough in our fight against depression. While some of us may not have been born into a supportive family, or we may not have lots of positive friends, nearly all of us know at least someone who makes us feel good, who encourages us and who is supportive of us. Seek these people out whenever you can and take on board the positive attitude and the encouragement they give you – you deserve it and it will help you fuel up with positive energy.

Supportive people help us through rough times.

6. Acknowledge Your Qualities and Skills

If we have a problem with depression and have low self-esteem, we tend to ignore and dismiss our positive qualities and abilities. Even if other people point out our good points, we often just shrug them off as being nothing special. We don't see the little things that others appreciate so much in us, such as reading a goodnight story to our child, or coaching a little league footy team. Being a good friend, loving partner, caring parent and contributor to society is something that should never be taken for granted, even by us.

By making a list of everything that is good about our life and us, we can build up self-esteem. For example we may have a loving partner who wouldn't be with us if we didn't deserve it, in other words we must have some loving qualities. Or we are skilled employees whose work is a big factor in the success of the company we work for. This list could go on and on. If we can't think of anything good about ourselves, we can ask our friends and family to tell us a few of our good points. We will be amazed at all the fabulous things they can say about us and how important we are in their lives. Every person has good points. The problem is we are the hardest people to convince of our own good qualities and skills. We should all chisel our strengths into stone, and put it in a prominent place where we can read it several times a day.

It is a good idea to make reminders of our positive qualities.

115

7. Learn How to Say "No" Without Feeling Guilty

It is a fact that when we are depressed we have a hard time standing up for ourselves and we often feel overwhelmed by the demands other people make on us. It is not uncommon that others take advantage of depressed people. This in turn only exacerbates the depression. Saying "no" without feeling guilty is sometimes the most difficult thing to do. It often seems that we would rather deal with an uncomfortable situation than say "no" to someone. Doing things we don't want to do, or putting up with things we don't want to put up with, doesn't help us build up our self-esteem. On the contrary, it makes us feel controlled by others.

Just because someone wants something from us, doesn't mean we have to come to the party. Saying "no" does not make us a bad person. We know our likes and dislikes best. Maybe the timing is wrong, or what has been asked for goes against our principles. Maybe agreeing to the other person's request might even be doing them a disservice. If we say yes we might take away their chance to be independent. Whatever the reason may be, we have a right to say "no". We owe it to ourselves to be true to ourselves and not let anyone bully us. We also don't necessarily need to justify our "no" either. Learning to say "no" is one of the most liberating actions.

We have the right to say no to something we don't want and we should not feel guilty about it

8. Make Positive Contributions to Others

Part of the CBT strategy in our effort to manage depression is to create as many good feelings as possible. Nothing makes us feel better faster than helping others. This is a classical Win-Win situation. If we make a positive contribution to others, be it donating to a charity, doing volunteer work, or mowing the lawn for an elderly person, we not only help someone in need, but we contribute to society. This makes us feel more valuable and it raises our self-esteem.

Turning our focus outwards occasionally will lift our spirits in no time and take our mind off our own problems. We can help at a charity, or lend a hand to someone who is struggling. We can even contribute to others while enjoying ourselves, if we are keen gardeners we can volunteer to replant native vegetation. If we love animals we can offer to walk the dogs at the local animal shelter. There are certainly plenty of opportunities to make a difference. However, this doesn't mean that we are obliged to constantly do things for others what they could do for themselves. Remember we can say "no". Also we should only give as much as we can afford, not having enough for oneself is counterproductive. When we look beyond our boundaries, there are many ways we can contribute to the wellbeing of others.

*Helping others not only supports our society
it also make us feel good.*

9. Involve Yourself in Activities You Enjoy

Unfortunately when we are depressed we first give up all those things we enjoy most. We seem to lose all enthusiasm for fun. Who hasn't heard the saying "all work and no play makes for a very dull day"? We cannot expect to maintain our bright outlook on life if we are only faced with obligations and nothing enjoyable in between. Even if we have to push ourselves in the beginning, we should at least do something enjoyable once a week. Having little rewarding breaks will increase our motivation to tackle the daily tasks. For a healthy self-esteem, we need to be able to look forward to some enjoyable activity. Playing is not only important for children, but also for adults.

People who occasionally take time out for themselves are much more relaxed and handle pressure better. Doing something enjoyable, be it working in the garden, reading a book or playing sport, will allow us to unwind and put the daily pressure aside for a while. Sometimes it even helps us to solve problems, because by doing something different, we step back and let our subconscious put the matter into a clearer perspective. It is also a good idea to take some time out and ponder over where you came from, where you are now and where you want to be in future. Looking after ourselves will promote our emotional balance and then we are better able to meet our obligations.

*Taking time out and doing something
we enjoy renews our energy.*

10. Take Action! — Do the Do!

Managing depression means that **WE** have to take the first step. It is time to get out of our comfy chair and start doing something about the things we want to change in our life. Be active! Only sitting around and thinking or talking about changing our life won't bring us out of the rut we are in. We need to back up our good intentions with actually doing something about them. We need to make things happen. Nobody else is going to do it for us. Instead of complaining what is wrong with our life, let us be the one to start making things right.

But don't try to tackle the big goals first and stay realistic about what you can achieve. The goal to lose 20 kgs in two weeks is firstly, not realistic and secondly, not healthy. Divide your goal into achievable mini goals, like losing a half a kilo per week. Start off slow and work yourself up to bigger and better things. Life rewards action and taking control of our life, regardless of the outcome, will make us feel better about ourselves. Let's shuffle those cards and start playing our hand. Sometimes we will get the desired result and sometimes we won't. But the experience is always worth it and very occasionally we may even end up with a result we would never have dreamt possible. We only lose if we don't try.

*Sometimes we need the proverbial kick in the backside
to get us going and do something about our life.*

Cookie Jar Activities

These are activities that are pleasant and make us feel better:

- laughing
- being relaxed
- eating good meals
- visualising a happy future
- enjoying a beautiful scenery
- having peace and quiet.

These activities are usually accompanied by emotions that are incompatible with being depressed. For example it is difficult to laugh and be depressed at the same time.

Here are some pleasant activities you can enjoy without any financial or emotional "cost":

Bushwalking

Enjoying the countryside

Listening to the sounds of nature

Gardening, landscaping

Sitting in the morning sun

Walking barefoot along a beach

Dancing

Singing or listening to music

Meditating

Reading a funny book or a joke book

etc.

* * *

Establishing a Support System

Human beings are basically social creatures. We like to live in groups and have frequent contact with other members of our species. However, in today's affluent society, single person households are on the increase and so is the occurrence of depression. Ironically, making contact with the world has never been so easy and efficient, yet more and more people are feeling isolated and lonely. It seems to be easier to talk with someone on the other side of the world, than it is with our next-door neighbour, or our family.

Whether we blame our ever increasing isolation on technology, or on the disintegration of the family unit, the fact remains that loneliness exacerbates depression. We need human contact and we need to feel integrated in a social structure. Social contact with other human beings increases our sense of belonging, our purpose in life and self-worth, and it promotes positive mental health. Establishing a social support network is vital for the management and recovery of depression. Each member of our support network helps us in different ways, and being able to rely on their support in difficult times can even be life saving.

How to Meet People

Invite acquaintances and friends for coffee, drinks, lunch or dinner. You could ask them to bring an interesting friend along, someone you don't know yet. Host a "Meet New Friends" party.

Take your dog for a walk in the park. A survey found that more than 50% of the pet owners surveyed said they met new friends as a direct result of their pet.

Do volunteer work or join an environmental, political, humanitarian or other cause. Working with others towards a goal you believe in, will establish strong, lasting relationships.

Join a hobby group. Find a nearby group with similar interest as yours. For example music, book, car clubs, gardening, crafts or sports group.

Go back to school. Take a college or community education course. Whether you are embarking on a new career or just widening your general knowledge, studying with other people is rewarding and establishes quality friendships.

Having various interests will bring you together with a wide variety of people and make you part of the community.

Family and Friends

Other people offer the best form of support. Family connections, friendships and being involved in social activities can act as buffers against stress, anxiety and depression. However, when we suffer from depression we often pull ourselves back from social activities, thereby isolating ourselves even more. This in turn only feeds the negative feelings and consequently deepens the depression. Depression is not something to be ashamed of, nor is it something we have done, and we have not been singled out because we are, or were, "bad". Depression can strike anyone, anytime, irrespective of background, intellect, education or wealth. If we are open with our family and friends about our depression, we will often be surprised at the amount of support we are offered.

It is important to establish a support network before we hit a crisis. We need to speak to our family and friends; tell them what we need when we are struggling with depressive thoughts. We can ask them what level of support they are able and willing to give us. Find out in which situations we can call on them and where their own boundaries lie. It is a good idea to make an Emergency Call List. Some of our friends and family may be able to offer support at any time, day or night. Others may themselves feel overwhelmed when we call them in a crisis situation. It is important to respect their caution and their willingness to acknowledge their limitations. They may be the ones to call when we just would like some company, or a pleasant chat about everyday things.

Many times we don't actually need to lean on our family and friends to reap the benefits. Often just knowing that someone is close by can lift us up and help us to make positive decisions. Developing and maintaining healthy social contact is a two-way street and involves give and take. There will be times when we are the ones giving support, and there will be times when we are receiving it. Making an effort to nurture our relationships with friends and family, like finding out what is happening in their lives, will ensure their support remains strong when we are going through a rough patch.

However, we must be wary of social support that can drain us. Maybe some people within our support circle are more demanding, or harmful, than supportive. These people may engage in unhealthy behaviours that we are trying to overcome, such as substance abuse. Or they may continually be negative, oppressive, or rigid. Such connections can be just as damaging as having no connections. In addition, we must also know our limits in giving social support to others. If our friends and family place too heavy demands on our time, resources and emotional strength, we may ourselves again become anxious and depressed because we feel we can't meet their needs.

As we are all different, our support systems will be different. Some people benefit from a large and diverse social support system; others prefer to confide in just a small group of family and friends. Which ever we choose, it helps to have people to turn to. That way, someone is always available when we are struggling with dark thoughts and need their support. Having several people to choose from also means that we don't overburden any one person.

Tips to cultivate friendships:

1) Go easy. Don't overwhelm new friends. Respect their boundaries.

2) Don't try to outdo your friends and don't practice one-upmanship. Let others also have their moment in the spotlight.

3) Adopt a healthy, realistic self-image. Both too much vanity as well as constant self-criticism can be very unattractive to potential friends.

4) Avoid nonstop complaining. Complaining about everybody and everything is tiresome, draining and depressing on friends.

5) Be fun to be with and try to find humour in everyday things.

Family and friends offer the best form of support.

Self-Help Groups

Another form of support are support groups, or Self-Help groups. A support group is a gathering of people who share a common condition or interest, such as depression. Most support groups meet on a regular basis. They can be a valuable addition to professional treatment. Support groups come in many forms. Some may be more structured and offer organised discussions and educational information. Maybe they have mental health professionals acting as guest speakers. Others may be more casual, preferring to concentrate on sharing personal experiences through informal talks.

How strongly we may want to participate is up to us. In the beginning, we may prefer to just listen and learn how others cope in similar situations. When we feel more comfortable in the group, then we may want to share some of our own experiences. Talking with people who know first-hand what it feels like to be depressed can be liberating. It makes us feel less alone and isolated. Good support groups are safe and welcoming environments, filled with understanding and compassionate people. They help reduce the stigma we may feel about having depression.

Through support groups we can improve our coping skills and make valuable connections. The other members of the group may offer encouragement so we feel more willing to get professional help and take an active part in the treatment of our depression. They motivate us when we feel like giving up. After all, they have been there and usually know the pitfalls and emotional desperation. Support groups can also help us tap into community resources for assistance, maybe for housing and transportation, or other social services. Members, who are more advanced in their treatment, may be willing to act as mentors for people just starting out on the road to recovery. Good support groups offer a wide range of benefits on emotional and practical levels.

There are a few points to be aware of when joining a support group. Support groups are not alternatives to professional treatment. Do not terminate treatment with your doctor, or mental health professional, because you've joined a support group. Also be wary about any information received regarding treatment and medications from other members of the group. People in support groups are fellow sufferers and not mental health professionals. They talk about their own experience, not about scientific facts. Also, do not stop taking your medication without consulting your doctor first and never be tempted to try out someone else's medication just to see how it works. Your doctor prescribes your medication and its dosage based on your physical and mental attributes, just as others get their medication based on their needs.

Where to Find Support Groups
There are various organisations and services that have a list of Support groups in your local area:

- Your family physician
- Local Council offices
- Mental health organisations and facilities
- Your local hospital
- Clinics and mental health professionals
- Telephone directory under community services
- Charity organsations such as Salvation Army
- Helplines
- Internet

In self-help groups you find like minded people who know exactly what you are going through, because they have experienced it themselves.

Social Groups, Churches and Special Interest Groups

Social groups, special interest groups or clubs, can be part of a support system. Often we just need to be in the company of people who are doing something that we like. Hobbies and sports may bring us together with people who are likeminded and with whom we can establish friendships. Taking part in social activities, or pursuing an interest with other people, gets us out of the house and helps us to integrate ourselves in a social structure. It also gives us a routine, and combats isolation and loneliness.

Many people turn to religion and other spiritual doctrines in times of emotional crises. Churches and religious gatherings can be invaluable pillars of support. Members of the clergy, pastors, priests and leaders of non-christian faiths often have some experience, if not training, in counselling. Offering support and advice is part of their professional agenda, and as outsiders to your situation, they may be able to provide a more objective point of view. They can address spiritual concerns and give reassurance in matters of faith. Sometimes churches and other religious organisations also provide other social services like emergency accommodation, access to medical and mental health services and mediation in conflict situations. Again, guidance by a spiritual leader does not replace professional therapy.

Church leaders are often experienced in counselling.

Pets and Animals

The companionship and unconditional love a pet gives its owner should never be underestimated. Nowadays doctors, therapists and other health professionals ask their patients about pet ownership. It has long been recognised that pets have a positive therapeutic effect on vulnerable people, especially with people who suffer from depression. Animals are the best listeners, and it doesn't matter if they don't understand the words, they sense the feelings. Being able to stroke soft fur or smooth feathers is immensly soothing. Pets have an extraordinary calming effect and are great antidotes against loneliness. Animals are often the only living creatures that can get through to a troubled mind and that we feel safe to love. Pets have saved countless lives by just being there.

Furthermore, being responsible and having to care for a pet can make us feel needed and give us a purpose in life. It also allows us to step back from our own problems and focus on something different. We experience a sense of value when meeting the needs of our pets. The daily routines involved in caring for an animal promote stability and safety. Sometimes the presence of a pet is the only calm thing in an otherwise emotionally turbulent environment. The concern over their pet's fate has persuaded many people not to take that final step and commit suicide. Their dog or cat was able to convince them that life was still worth living. Keep in mind that a pet requires a longterm committment. Be sure you can honour it before getting an animal.

Animals seem to be able to empathise with human suffering.

In recent times numerous support sites and forums for depression and mental illness have appeared on the Internet and become very popular. Although these sites can be a helpful source of support and the anonymity is certainly appealing, it can also be deceptive. The people you're interacting with may not be who they say they are. So be careful about divulging personal details such as address and financial details. Be also wary if you are encouraged to stop treatment, or you are asked to buy certain products. Joining an internet forum for depression may give you access to support 24 hours a day, seven days a week, but you must not to let the extensive Internet contact lead to isolation from your in-person social network.

Having healthy relationships not only helps to alleviate depression, but also helps to prevent its recurrence. Isolation, on the other hand, makes us more vulnerable to mental and physical problems. It can be hard to overcome depression by oneself. Having a social support network will help us come through the depressive episodes better. It is never too late to build and/or rebuild friendships or choose to become involved. The investment in social support will pay off in better health and a brighter outlook for years to come.

* * *

How to Prevent Relapsing into Depression

In order to prevent a relapse into depression it is important to firstly acknowledge that we suffer from depression. Unless we accept that we have a problem with depression, it will be difficult to constructively confront the negative issues that our depression causes. Many people use denial as a way of not having to deal with their depression. This is an unconscious psychological process people apply when their comfort zone is threatened. Even though this zone may be one that is painful and destructive, it can still be "comfortable" and familiar and people may still use denial to avoid dealing with the situation. Although denial may temporarily protect us, it blocks our awareness of our own self-destructive behaviour and the negative impact it has on our lives.

Denial masquerades in many disguises. Simple denial is when we argue that something that is real, is not real: that we are not depressed, when we really are. Another form of denial is minimising the effect that the depression has on our daily lives and our personal relationships. Or we blame someone else for our behaviour and thereby refuse to accept responsibility for ourselves. We might rationalise our behaviour with countless excuses and justifications or intellectualise the problem and deal with it only in an abstract and theoretical way, thus avoiding any emotional involvement. We need to acknowledge our depression and work at it every day.

*Acknowledging that you have depression will help
to constructively confront the problems it causes.*

Work with Your Doctor or Mental Health Professional

To avoid a relapse into depression it is paramount that we establish a good working relationship with our doctor or therapist. If you don't have a doctor it would be wise to inform your family doctor of your depressive feelings. He or she can provide short-term support and refer you to a specialist if needed. It is important that we educate our doctor about ourselves. We must tell him or her about our medical problems. Our doctor must know about any other medications we are taking, including over the counter and recreational drugs and also our alcohol consumption.

Taking an active part in our healing is vital for managing our depression. The best results are achieved by those who take control of their depression and consult frequently with their physician or health care worker. If we have any questions, we must ask them, and remember there really is no such thing as a dumb question. If we are unhappy with our physician's advice, or unsure about something, we can discuss it with him or her openly. We need to explain exactly what it is that we don't like, or don't understand and what we expect. A good doctor will welcome the opportunity to talk through any problems and clarify misunderstandings. If that doesn't work, we can always get a second opinion.

Your doctor is your partner in the
management process of your depression.

Inform Yourself about Your Depression

Unless we have some understanding of our depression it will be difficult to accept it and do something about it. It is important to ask your doctor or therapist to explain the depressive feelings to you. How long you can expect a downturn to last and what are the symptoms that you are likely to experience? Apart from your physician or mental health care professional, there are many other sources where you can get information about depression. The Internet has many excellent sites explaining depression and other mental health problems. The bookshop, or local library, will most likely have books and other material on the subject.

The Diagnostic and Statistical Manual of Mental Disorders (DSM-IV-TR) is the book used by many doctors and other mental health professionals to diagnose mental illnesses. It describes the symptoms of the different mental disorders in detail. Any library associated with a university will have, or be able to get, the DSM-IV-TR. And of course, this book is an excellent introduction for sufferers and carers alike to understanding depressive disorders. Knowledge is one of the best defences against a relapse into depression. The better we know our depression and its symptoms, the earlier we can recognise a problem and take pre-emptive action.

*If we inform ourself about depression
we will be able to cope with it better.*

Take Your Medicine as Directed by Your Doctor

Do not increase, or decrease your medication without direction by your doctor. If you miss a dose, don't double up; if you miss several doses, consult your doctor. Some medications take several weeks before the full benefit is noticed. Do not get discouraged if you don't feel better immediately. When you are feeling better, do not stop taking your medication. Feeling good does not mean you no longer have depression. It is simply a sign that the medication is working and to keep on feeling good, you must regularly take the medicine as directed until your doctor tells you to stop.

Do not mix your medication with other drugs without consulting your doctor first. Avoid taking prohibited street drugs, (Marijuana, Heroin, Ecstasy, amphetamines, etc), as these affect your mind. Your medication is prescribed to stabilise your mood and psychoactive drugs, street drugs (not over the counter drugs such as Aspirin or paracetamol) and alcohol, can upset the chemical balance in your brain. This can have a negative effect on your emotions and drastically alter your moods. Ask your doctor to explain how your medication works, the dosage and frequency of taking it. Understanding your medication is an important part in preventing a relapse.

Taking the medication as prescribed is vital in the management of depression.

Get to Know the Side Effects of Your Medication and How to Manage Them

Most medications have some unwanted effects. These may range from minor discomfort to serious unpleasantness. When your doctor prescribes the medication, ask about the side effects that you can expect and how high the probability is that you may encounter them. Every person experiences side effects differently; some people may have none, while others may be severely affected. Learn to recognise the side effects and discuss with your doctor how you can deal with them and what your tolerance level would be.

Side effects are often the major reason why people suffering from depression stop taking their medication, which in turn causes a relapse. However, if we know what to expect, we are more capable of dealing with the situation. Some side effects may only occur at the start of taking the medication. As soon as the body has adjusted to the medication, they often subside. Common side effects might include dry mouth, nausea, sleepiness, dizziness or light-headedness. Less common side effects include muscle spasms, shakes, stiffness and restlessness. There are particular interventions for different side-effects, so be sure to notify your doctor. For example, physical activity, such as exercise, may reduce the severity of some of these side effects. The better you are informed about possible side-effects, the better you will be able to cope with them.

If we know what side effects to expect we can better deal with them.

133

Get Involved in Life

Start getting involved in life, become active and do things you enjoy. Combat loneliness and isolation by building new friendships. Say hello to the neighbours and have a chat with your local greengrocer. Sometimes pleasant small talk is all you need to put you in the right frame of mind for the day. At other times, you may need a strong shoulder to lean on. Build yourself a support system of friends that you can call when the going gets tough. It is advisable to develop at least one close friend with whom you can talk about your thoughts and feelings. Friends sometimes recognise changes in our behaviour much earlier than we do. These changes may signal that you need to see your doctor.

Become physical and start moving your body. Go for walks, join a gymnasium or start weeding the garden. It is scientifically shown that exercise has a beneficial effect on our mood. It increases the level of serotonin in our brain, which makes us feel good. Exercise motivates us and gives us more energy. We often feel better for having accomplished an activity, and develop a sense of capability. Also, getting in shape and toning our body will be good for our self-esteem and lift our mood. With an ever-increasing sedentary lifestyle, regular exercise is becoming more and more important for our physical and mental wellbeing.

It is scientifically proven that physical activity helps lift our depression.

Be Kind to Yourself

Just as it has taken time for your depression to establish itself in your life it will also take time for you to get control over it and work towards a recovery. Even feeling better can be scary at first and you need to adjust to it. We may have become used to being enclosed by the walls of depression and even felt a sense of safety in our despair. Now suddenly the familiar painful feelings are dwindling and we have to learn to replace them with something that feels good, or at least not painful.

It isn't our fault that we have a problem with depression and we didn't choose it. But we can choose if we are going to continue to let depression exert its damaging influence on us. It is primarily our responsibility to take back control of our life. We can't shove the ball into someone else's corner and wait for them to treat us differently or for situations to change and hope for the best. CBT has taught us that because of the depression we inadvertently created negative situations and other people responded to how we related to them. The circumstances of our life will not change unless we change our behaviour.

There will be times when you think you are taking one step forward and two steps back. It is very important that you are patient and gentle with yourself. Managing depression works on the same principles as learning to manage an addiction. We take it slowly, one day at a time. Sometimes even one hour at a time. If we can feel good for half an hour today we are already making progress. Maybe tomorrow or next week we will feel all right for one or two hours per day. If we make a daily effort to recognise and deal with the depressive automatic thoughts and core beliefs, we will gradually lengthen the times we feel all right, or even feel good, and reduce the down times. The progress may at first seem painstakingly slow, but if we persevere and keep on monitoring our thoughts, it will steadily increase. Soon the good times will become the norm and the depressive episodes will become the exception.Most important of all you will have learnt that the depressive feelings will eventually go away. There is relief in sight.

With the depression lifting, you will able to deal with life and all its ups and downs more efficiently and most likely have energy left over to do some of the things you really enjoy. Also you will be a lot more fun to be around.

Your progress has positive effects on your loved ones, your friends and society in general. Actually having learnt to manage depression in a positive manner will make you a valuable friend and role model. Other people who are grappling with depressive feelings can look to you for support and understanding. Controlling the dark shadow of depression will help you become the person you want to be.

YOU CAN DO IT

CPSIA information can be obtained
at www.ICGtesting.com
Printed in the USA
LVIW011514280812

296369LV00001B